The Easy

Tree
Guide

The Easy
Tree
Guide

Keith Rushforth

Paintings by Gill Tomblin
and Ann Winterbotham

Britain and Europe

AURUM PRESS

First published in Great Britain 2001 by Arum Press Limited,
25 Bedford Avenue, London WC1B 3AT

© Duncan Petersen Publishing Ltd 2001
© Keith Rushforth 2001

A catalogue record for this book is available from the British Library

ISBN 1 85410 750 X

Originated by Mick Hodson Associates
Printed in Italy by Printer Trento S.r.l.

Conceived, edited, designed and produced by
Duncan Petersen Publishing, 31, Ceylon Road, London W14 0PY

Editorial Director
Andrew Duncan
Art Director
Mel Petersen

Text by
Keith Rushforth

Paintings by
Gill Tomblin and Ann Winterbotham

Photographs provided by
Frank Lane Picture Agency, Harry Smith Horticultural Photographic Collection, Ken Ashburner

Editorial Assistants
Nicola Davies
Mark Adcock
Design Assistants
Beverly Stewart
Christopher Foley

Contents

About this book

CAN A TREE GUIDE *REALLY* BE EASY?

Yes: trees are readily identified – with the right information to hand – because they can be examined at leisure. It's also helpful that they provide identification features ('characters') throughout the year. While it is true that trees are easier to identify at some times than others, if needs must, you can tell tree from tree at any season.

Perhaps the main problem people have with tree identification is the variability of trees; and that sometimes (especially in woodland), the leaves are out of reach.

HOW EASY?

In making this *the* easy tree guide we have concentrated on several key points:

■ **The photographs are, for a tree field guide, uniquely large and clear, a**nd designed to work hand in hand with the **paintings** (the artwork). For maximum ease of comparison, they face each other on opposite pages of each double page spread in the guide.

Photographs can't be equalled for an overall impression of a tree; while the artwork panel highlights the details essential for identification, and allows comparison with other species. You'll find it valuable to let your eyes roam between the two, associating details in the artwork panel with the whole tree.

Typical barks are shown in separate small photographs, another very useful feature.

■ **Simple language** The text is an easy read for anyone, avoiding jargon and technical terms. The captions in the artwork panel highlight the key identification features of the paintings.

■ **Important variations** are described in the captions to the artwork and to the photographs.

■ **The distribution** and **preferred habitat** of each species are described in the main text under the artwork panel.

THE APPEAL OF TREES

Trees stir the emotions, whether we want to embrace them, or to chop them down. They are large, and can appear to live forever. They make landmarks and meeting places; they give character to our towns and they play a major role in defining our landscapes. They cause problems, such as shading houses and cutting out sunlight; they drop debris and harbour pests such as squirrels and pigeons. They are useful, not just for timber and firewood, but because they shade our houses, brighten our gardens with their flowers and fruits; and provide homes for many a creature, including squirrels and pigeons. Genesis chapter 2, verse 9, sums it up in simplistic, but timeless, Biblical style: trees are *'pleasing to the eye and good for food'*. At times we may love them or hate them, but we can't ignore them.

Although there are many more trees in Europe than can be covered in these pages, this guide does feature all the commonest trees in Western, Northern, Central and Southern Europe – and more. If you need a guide that covers every single tree seen in Europe, see the reading list on page 288.

Keith Rushforth AUTUMN 2000

Technical terms

In this guide, technical terms are accompanied by a simple definition in (we hope) plain English. This glossary offers a somewhat fuller explanation of terms used, as well as covering some additional botanical terms in common use.

alternate: leaves or buds that emerge first one side of a twig, then the other

annual shoot: the growth made in a single year.

aril: fleshy or juicy base to a fruit, see yew (p48-49)

auriculate: with ear-like lobes.

bastard: hybrid between two species.

bole: trunk of a tree.

bract: structure (derived from a leaf) beneath a flower or fruit. It can be leafy, but not necessarily.

capsule: a dry fruit with two or more cells, and which opens when ripe.

catkin: male or female flower without petals – often their pollen spreads on the wind. Usually hangs down.

cluster: where several parts occur together.

crown: upper part of a tree which has the leaves.

decussate: leaves in opposite pairs, with the alternate pairs at right angles to the pair above and below.

digitate: with finger-like leaflets from a common point.

dioecious: with male and female flowers on separate trees.

drupe: fruit in which the seed is protected by a stony layer, outside which is a fleshy covering (eg, a cherry).

fascicle (of needles): bundle of needles

foliage: leaves and twigs

habit: overall form or growth pattern.

heterosis: extra vigour shown by a hybrid.

lamina: blade or flat part of leaf.

lanceolate: lance-shaped

leaflets: separate divisions of a compound leaf

leaf veins: veins in leaf which transport water and nutrients.

linear (of leaves): a narrow, straight leaf

lobe: projection on leaf margin - may be round or pointed..

long shoot: the opposite of a short shoot, and only significant on trees which have short shoots, for example larch and cedars.

needle: leaf of a conifer, often but not always sharp

net-veined: when the veins form a visible network on a leaf.

obovate: egg-shaped but broadest above the middle

opposite: buds or leaves arranged in pairs on twig.

ovate: egg-shaped but broadest below the middle

palmate: with veins or leaflets starting from the end of the leaf stalk

petiole: leaf stalk

panicle: a branched, compound flower head (inflorescence) with many individual flowers.

paripinnate: pinnate, with an even number of pairs of leaflets.

pinnate: compound leaf where the leaflets arise successively from a central stalk

pioneer species: the first to grow (colonise) a bare site.

pod: fruit of a legume, such as a pea.

phyllode: a shoot modified to act as a leaf.

radial: like bicycle spokes

scale leaf small leaf of some conifers, see cypress family

shoot: extension growth.

short shoot: which lengthens a little each year.

stamen: male parts of a flower, with an anther or pollen-producing part at the tip

stipule: growth similar to leaf, but not a leaf, at base of leaf stalk

style: female part of a flower, with pollen-receiving **stigma** at the tip

sucker: shoot growing directly from a root or base of trunk.

symbiosis: when two dissimilar organisms live together.

toothed: small, irregular points on leaf margin.

unisexual: of a single sex (most flowers contain both male and female parts).

verticillate: in whorls. A whorl is a number of parts occur together at more or less the same points.

About this book

What is a tree?

This apparently simple question is surprisingly difficult to answer precisely. A tree must have a woody stem, but so must a shrub. The defining factor, then, must be ability to grow to a large size. But how large is 'large'? In this guide, our watershed is 5 m; below that, it's generally safe to consider it a shrub. Most of the trees featured in this guide can grow to 15 m or more, and some will grow to 60 m in a favourable place; but a few common trees, such as rowan, are usually around 10 m when fully grown.

Naming trees

All trees have several names, and these fall into two main categories: common names and scientific (or Latin) names. Common names are extremely variable, and frequently confusing. Rowan is often called mountain ash, but has nothing to do with the true ashes (apart from the superficial similarity of the leaves) and grows in lowland woodland as well as up mountains. Box elder is more confusing, being neither a box (*Buxus*, a group of shrubs and small trees not covered in the guide); nor an elder (see page 281); it is, in fact, a maple.

Botany uses a unique Latin name for each species, recognized the world over. It consists of two parts: the first part, the genus, describes its immediate group: *Sorbus* and *Acer* are both genus names. The second part is the specific name, such as *aucuparia* for rowan and *negundo* for box elder. This pins it down to one particular species. In botany, there can be only a single genus with the same name and in each genus there can be only one species with any one specific name. However, the same specific name can be used in another genus. Examples in this guide include *Abies alba* in the silver firs and *Populus alba* in the poplars (*alba* means white); or *Morus nigra*, *Pinus nigra* and *Populus nigra* (*nigra* means black). The specific name often tells you something about the plant: for instance, *Pterocarya fraxinifolia* translates as the 'wing nut with ash-like leaves'.

Despite Latin names being unique, a tree may get two or more of them. However, the oldest validly published name has precedence, and the newer names rank as synonyms. Some common synonyms are given in the index.

Although not important in an easy tree guide, botany ranks all species in a hierarchy. Individual species are essentially the lowest 'rank' – though subspecies, varieties or forms are one lower. Next up from species are the genera (plural of genus*)*; genera are placed in families (for instance, willows and poplars are in the *Salicaceae* or willow family); and families are placed in orders. The conifers in this guide belong to several families (*Araucariaceae, Cupressaceae, Pinaceae* and *Taxodiaceae*) but all belong to one order, *Coniferales*, except for the yews or *Taxus*, which are always placed in their own family, *Taxaceae* and often in their own order, the *Taxales*. Likewise gingko or maidenhair tree, which has its own family, *Ginkgoaceae* and order, *Ginkgoales*.

Next up in the hierarchy, above order, comes 'class'. There are two classes: *Gymnospermae*, literally 'naked seeds'; and *Angiospermae*, literally 'hidden seeds'. This last is divided into two subclasses, *Dicotyledoneae* (having two seed leaves and secondary thickening of stems) and the *Monocotyledoneae* (having one seed leaf and lacking the capacity to make secondary thickening). *Dicotyledoneae* (frequently shortened to '*Dicots*') include all the broadleaved trees; and *Monocotyledoneae* (shortened to Monocots) include the palms (also grasses and orchids). Both contain many orders and families.

Finding a tree – through the index

Any tree in the guide can of course be reached via the index, pages 284-288, listing both scientific and common names. As you become more familiar with trees, you will use the index increasingly. But, however efficient an index may be, it is useless if you don't know the tree's name in the first place.

FINDING A TREE – IF YOU DON'T KNOW ITS NAME

If you're starting from scratch – typically with a twig and some leaves gathered on a walk – simply browse through the book, comparing what you have with the artwork and photographs. With more than 270 pages to get through, this might seem a daunting task; but it's not as difficult as you might think

The order in which the species fall is designed to help. It groups them according to leaf shape. The book starts with ginkgo (pages 14-15) and monkey puzzle (pages 16-17): special cases which are best got out of the way first. Then the remainder of the conifers follow in a logical order: those with small scale-like leaves come first (pages 18-35); then trees with 'needle' leaves (pages 36-81) and finally the pines (pages 82-101), with needle leaves in bundles of two to five.

Hiba: small scale-like leaves.

Below, deodar cedar: needle leaves.

Above, stone pine: needle leaves in bundles.

The broadleaved section starts with trees that have simple leaves (pages 106-237). In this section, related trees are generally placed together, but leaves with small lobes come first, followed by those with large lobes; however, alder and birch, with toothed (not lobed) leaves come right at the beginning and the trees with more strongly lobed leaves, such as sycamore, at the end.

> **Introductions to conifers and broadleaves, pages 12-13 and 102-105**
> These two spreads can speed up the process of getting to roughly the right page of the guide. They are a visual key, breaking down the contents into groups whose foliage looks roughly similar.

Even this order is not absolute: for instance, white poplar (pages 134-135) is placed with the other poplars, despite its strongly lobed leaves.

Black popular: simple leaves.

The broadleaved trees with compound, pinnate leaves (divided into leaflets) are on pages 240-271, with horse

Sycamore: strongly lobed.

chestnuts (leaves compound, but like a palm's) as a one-off on pages 272-273. The palms, with their immense compound leaves, are on pages 274-279.

A short final section, pages 280-283, has brief entries on a selection of shrubs, or shrub-like trees.

> **The main text descriptions**
> These always start with information on the tree's native range – those parts of the world (often far from Europe) where it grows naturally. The rest of the text deals with the tree as Europeans will find it . To avoid repetition, the fact that trees have been much transported into Europe from around the world and naturalized here is taken as understood.

Features that identify trees

This guide uses obvious identification features or characters rather than detailed botanical ones. (This explains some of the ordering, such as box elder (*Acer negundo*) being placed with the pinnate-leaved trees (pages 240-241) and several pages after the other maples. Trees, like other higher plants ('higher' as opposed to the 'lower' plants, such as ferns, mosses and liverworts), have stems with bark, shoots, buds, leaves, flowers and fruits and these are the characters which the guide describes.

Height and silhouette.

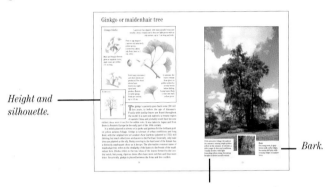

Bark.

Main photo caption.

Height and silhouette The height range of an average mature tree is given in the small panel on the left-hand page of each spread, below the main artwork panel. Here you will also see a silhouette of the tree, emphasizing its typical outline. For evergreen trees (most conifers and some broadleaves), the silhouettes are of course the same all year; for deciduous trees, the winter silhouette, without foliage, is given.

Bark This can be very informative and diagnostic, but is also variable between individuals of the same species; and it changes enormously as a tree matures. The small photographs on the right-hand page of each spread generally show the bark of a mature tree, with the caption describing changes as the tree matures.

The main photo captions describe the tree's crown shape – the crown being the top part of a tree, carrying the foliage. Crowns, like bark, vary considerably.

Shoots and buds The colour and texture of shoots can be very useful for identification: see, for example, Norway maple (page 228) and Cappadocian maple (page 230). Shoot colour when described refers to the mature shoot from late summer.

The arrangement of the buds and leaves also provides useful clues. Three quarters of all broadleaved trees have them alternate along the shoot; on the rest they are in opposite pairs, apart from a few where they are in threes. Buds tend to be concentrated at the tips of shoots and the number of protective bud scales can also be a useful feature.

Beech: alternate on the shoot.

Rowan: pinnate leaves.

Obovate.

which end of an egg is the bottom, but in botany the question is decided: normal egg-shaped is **ovate**, and defined as being broadest below the middle (i.e. broad end attached); while leaves which are egg-shaped but broadest above the middle are **obovate** (i.e. narrow end attached).

Ovate.

Leaves are the easiest characters of all. Leaf shape varies widely, with **pinnate** and **bi-pinnate** or twice-pinnate leaves at one extreme and simple **untoothed** leaves at the other. (Pinnate means divided into leaflets.) Some trees change leaf shape as the tree matures – see juvenile holm oak (page 152) and holly (page 216).

Pear: untoothed leaves.

Leaf stalk or petiole.

At first glance, a pinnate leaf can look like a shoot with many leaves. However, there are always buds in the angle or **axil** formed between a true leaf and a shoot, but see swamp cypress (page 44) and dawn redwood (page 42).

The shape of simple leaves can vary from narrow and straight (**linear**), as in many conifers and some willows, to broader egg-shaped leaves, to leaves with marked toothing or **lobing**. The main teeth and lobes are often the ends of the lateral veins on the leaf, and leaves which have no teeth are often not as heavily veined.

The term egg-shaped appears frequently in this guide to describe not just the leaves, but also some fruits. Gulliver (in Swift's *Gulliver's Travels*) may have had trouble working out

Ginko flowers.

Check with the artwork to see whether the 'egg-shape' is ovate or obovate.

The **leaf stalk** or petiole can also provide valuable characters, such as most cherries (pages 180-185) and London plane (page 222).

Flowers These can be very obvious when doing their stuff, which is to attract attention. However, in many trees they are rather transient, or only produced on older trees or at the tops of tall trees.

Fruits These also provide very useful characters. The fruit is present from the fertilization of the flower until it matures and is shed. The descriptions given provide details of the fruit, including how it changes as it ripens.

Sweet gum: lobed leaves.

A key to conifers

Austrian pine.

Conifer means 'bearing cones' – and cone refers both to the overall shape of the tree, and its fruit. But although most conifers have obvious cones and cone-shaped crowns, many do not. From a scientific viewpoint, what really defines conifers is the seeds or ovules: they are naked – in other words, not enclosed within a protective structure. This can be seen very easily with a handlens in the female flowers of the cypresses. At the flowering stage, the small dot-like ovules are exposed between the small scales. After pollination, the scales expand and hide them. Other conifers make a better job of hiding them, even at the flowering stage, but they are always exposed to the air. This is a clear contrast with the broadleaved trees and palms, whose ovules are fully enclosed within the plant's tissues.

The conifers are an old and very diverse group, especially when ginkgo is treated as an honorary member: it actually belongs, botanically, between the ferns and the conifers.

The majority of conifers are evergreen, but larch (page 50), dawn redwood (page 42), swamp cypress (page 44) and ginkgo (page 14-15) are deciduous. Generally, they have single trunks and light branching, forming wood which is soft and strong. This makes them desirable for timber.

Pages 14-15
Ginkgo family
Leaves broadest at the rounded tip and with many parallel veins

Pages 16-17
Monkey puzzle family
Leaves broad at the base with a sharp point. Cones have a single seed fused to the supporting scale.

Monkey puzzle.

Juniper.

Pages 18-37
Cypress family
Leaves generally scale like, but some juniper species (pages 34-37) have straight and narrow (linear) leaves in whorls.
The family divides into three groups on cone characters:

Cones with shield-like (peltate) scales, i.e. scales which have a central stalk – *Cupressus* (pages 18-26) and *Chamacyparis* (pages 24-27).

Shield-like scales.

Hinged at base.

Cones with few scales hinged at the base – *Calocedrus* (pages 28-29), *Thuja* (pages 30-31), and *Thujopsis* (pages 32-33).

Cone a fleshy
berry, not woody
– *Juniperus*
(pages 34-37).

Coastal redwood.

Spanish juniper.

Pages 38-47
Redwood family
Leaves in flat
sprays .

Pages 48-49
Yew family
Leaves in flat
sprays and fruit
single, with a
juicy red base
(aril).
   (The yew family is
placed here on visual
foliage character.
Botanically, it belongs between ginkgo
and monkey puzzle.)

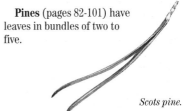

Yew.

Pages 50-101
Pine family
A large and important group, in which
there are two seeds to each cone scale.
It consists of:

Larches (pages 50-53)
and cedars (pages 54-
57) whose leaves are
on short spur shoots.
Cones of larch are
persistent, whereas in
cedars the mature
cone disintegrates to
release the seeds and
bracts.

Cedar of Lebanon.

Douglas fir.

Spruces (pages
58-67), Douglas
fir (pages 68-69),
silver firs (pages
70-77) and
hemlock (pages
80-81), whose
foliage is in
sprays with
single needle
leaves. Cones of silver firs break apart to
scatter the seeds.
   Spruces, Douglas fir and hemlock
have cones which are woody and
persistent.

   Pines (pages 82-101) have
leaves in bundles of two to
five.

Scots pine.

Yew.

Ginkgo or maidenhair tree

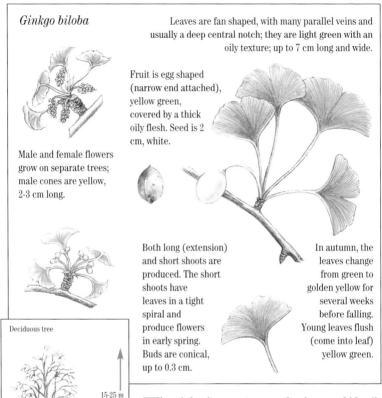

Ginkgo biloba

Leaves are fan shaped, with many parallel veins and usually a deep central notch; they are light green with an oily texture; up to 7 cm long and wide.

Fruit is egg shaped (narrow end attached), yellow green, covered by a thick oily flesh. Seed is 2 cm, white.

Male and female flowers grow on separate trees; male cones are yellow, 2-3 cm long.

Both long (extension) and short shoots are produced. The short shoots have leaves in a tight spiral and produce flowers in early spring. Buds are conical, up to 0.3 cm.

In autumn, the leaves change from green to golden yellow for several weeks before falling. Young leaves flush (come into leaf) yellow green.

Deciduous tree

15-25 m

The ginkgo's ancestry goes back some 200 million years, to before the age of dinosaurs. Fossils with similar leaves are found throughout the world. It is now only native to a remote region of eastern China and probably would have become extinct there were it not for the edible nuts. It was taken to Japan and from there to Western Europe in the early part of the 18th century.

It is widely planted in streets or in parks and gardens for the brilliant golden yellow autumn foliage. Ginkgo is tolerant of urban conditions and long lived, with the original tree at London's Kew Gardens (planted in 1762) still thriving; but much older trees are known in the Far East. Generally, only male trees are planted as the oily, fleshy covering to the hard seed of the female has a distinctly unpleasant odour as it decays. The alternative common name of maidenhair tree refers to the similarity of the leaves to the fronds of the maidenhair fern. *Biloba* refers to the two lobes of the leaves formed by the central notch, but young, vigorous trees often have more notches and thus more lobes. Botanically, ginkgo is placed between the ferns and the conifers.

With attractive foliage throughout the summer, turning bright golden yellow in the autumn, it tolerates a wide range of sites and conditions. Usually slender, with light branching when young, becoming broader in their second century.

BARK
On young trees, is grey brown with corky ridges, becoming dull grey with crossing ridges on mature trees.

15

Monkey puzzle

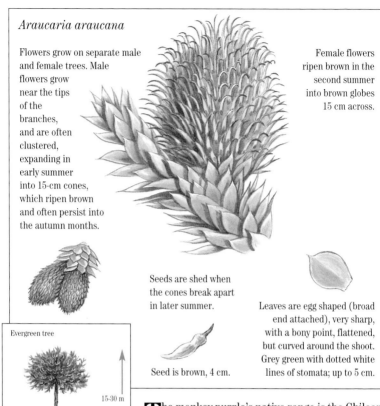

Araucaria araucana

Flowers grow on separate male and female trees. Male flowers grow near the tips of the branches, and are often clustered, expanding in early summer into 15-cm cones, which ripen brown and often persist into the autumn months.

Female flowers ripen brown in the second summer into brown globes 15 cm across.

Seeds are shed when the cones break apart in later summer.

Seed is brown, 4 cm.

Leaves are egg shaped (broad end attached), very sharp, with a bony point, flattened, but curved around the shoot. Grey green with dotted white lines of stomata; up to 5 cm.

Evergreen tree

15-30 m

The monkey puzzle's native range is the Chilean Andes between 37 and 39 degrees south, and in adjacent parts of the Argentinean Andes. In Britain and Europe, it is planted as a specimen tree mainly because of its distinctive shape.

The name monkey puzzle was given at a ceremonial planting in the 1840s, and alludes to the sharp foliage, which would puzzle a climbing monkey. Araucarias were around long before monkeys, however, and date from the Jurassic period otherwise dominated by the dinosaurs. An alternative name for the species is Chile pine.

The seeds (only carried on female trees, where there is a male within pollinating distance) are very tasty, especially if roasted. The Latin name refers to the Araucano Indians, for whom the seeds were an important food source. The timber is of a high-quality.

This tree is most unusual amongst conifers in being able to make suckers from the roots: old specimens are sometimes seen with a grove of suckers around them or on one side.

On young trees, the branching is in a whorls, giving an open conical appearance, but as the trees age they become rounded at the top and denser. When growing on dry sites and where the foliage is shaded, the lower branches are lost. The bold, whorled foliage makes these unlike any other trees. They do not associate well with other species, and do best either as isolated specimens, or in groves.

BARK
Grey or dark grey, with horizontal wrinkles which have been compared to an elephant's hide. But it may be fissured.

Italian cypress

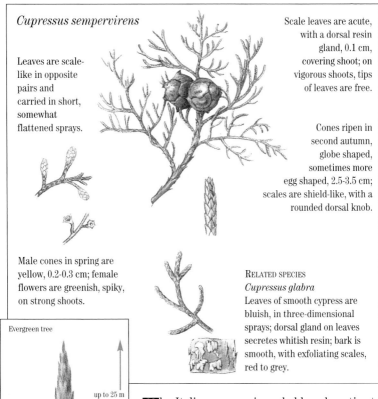

Cupressus sempervirens

Leaves are scale-like in opposite pairs and carried in short, somewhat flattened sprays.

Scale leaves are acute, with a dorsal resin gland, 0.1 cm, covering shoot; on vigorous shoots, tips of leaves are free.

Cones ripen in second autumn, globe shaped, sometimes more egg shaped, 2.5-3.5 cm; scales are shield-like, with a rounded dorsal knob.

Male cones in spring are yellow, 0.2-0.3 cm; female flowers are greenish, spiky, on strong shoots.

RELATED SPECIES
Cupressus glabra
Leaves of smooth cypress are bluish, in three-dimensional sprays; dorsal gland on leaves secretes whitish resin; bark is smooth, with exfoliating scales, red to grey.

Evergreen tree

up to 25 m

The Italian cypress is probably only native to the eastern Mediterranean region through to Iran. The wild form has horizontal short spreading branches. The most commonly planted form is var. *stricta*. which has erect branches making a very narrow-crowned tree, typical of regions such as Tuscany. In the wild, the tree is characteristic of limestone areas, and tolerant of long, hot dry summers. It is susceptible to a fungal disease (*Corynium* canker). This enters the scale leaves and kills the fine shoots and often larger branches. In severe cases, the tree is killed, but more often only large parts of the crown, rendering the tree unattractive, but alive. Cypresses have hard, fine wood, but it is usually not available in sufficient lengths or quantities to be commercially useful.

Smooth cypress is a tree from central Arizona. It is planted as an amenity tree for its blue-grey foliage and attractive bark. The dorsal resin glands rupture and secrete resin, which dries to a grey-white colour. The cones are 1.7-2.3 cm in length and the scales have forward-pointing prickles.

The 'wild' form has short spreading branches and makes a column-shape when mature, but the variety *stricta*, shown here, with its very narrow tight crown of erect branches, is more commonly planted.

BARK
Grey-brown developing scaly ridges which are usually set at an angle and spiral up the trunk.

Monterey cypress

Cupressus macrocarpa

Cones, 2-4 cm, ripen in second autumn but persist on tree; scales are shield-like, lumpy with a small transverse ridge.

Foliage is in dense three-dimensional sprays, which are carried erect or spreading; leaves are scale-like, 0.2 cm, in opposite pairs which cover the shoot. They are green and acute at the tip, which is pressed down on the shoot. Dorsal resin gland is very faint and does not secrete resin.

RELATED SPECIES

Cupressus nootkatensis

Nootka cypress has foliage in flattened, drooping, possibly pendulous sprays, maybe 0.5 m in length. Scale leaves come in slightly unequal pairs, with the facing pair slightly shorter than the lateral pair. They are dark green, with a free bony point; dorsal resin gland is faint or absent.

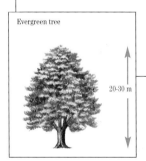

Evergreen tree

20-30 m

Nootka cypress cones ripen in spring to summer of second year, globular, up to 1.2 cm, with four to six pairs of scales with strong, recurved spines.

The Monterey cypress is restricted in the wild to two small coastal areas on the Monterey peninsula of California, where the trees are small and stunted by the wind. Old trees develop very wide spreading crowns on level, tiered branches, and from a distance look similar to mature cedars of Lebanon. The combination of bright green foliage and the relatively large cones distinguish it from similar species. It is susceptible to *Corynium* canker and is usually disfigured by dead areas in the crown. The wood is resistant to decay, but not particularly strong and not usually available in marketable quantities.

Nootka cypress has a wide distribution from Northern California to southern Alaska, occurring as a mountain species. It makes a much larger tree in the wild, up to 40 m, with bole diameters to nearly 3 m and produces a quality timber. It has been placed in the genus *Chamaecyparis*, but fits better in *Cupressus* and, as in this genus, the cones ripen in the second year (as opposed to the first year in *Chamaecyparis*). In cultivation, Nootka cypress is mainly found as very neat conical to broad conical trees.

Young trees are conical and rather spiky, but mature trees often become very flat topped and wide spreading.

BARK
Pale brown and finely ridged on young trees, maturing pink brown to grey and developing shallow cross-ridging on old trees.

Leyland cypress

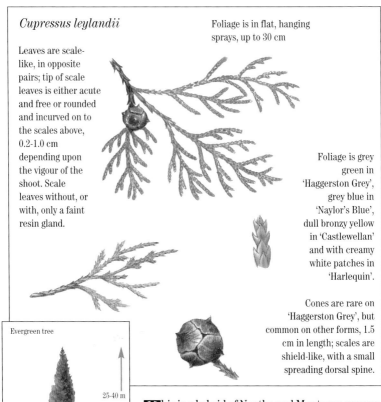

Cupressus leylandii

Foliage is in flat, hanging sprays, up to 30 cm

Leaves are scale-like, in opposite pairs; tip of scale leaves is either acute and free or rounded and incurved on to the scales above, 0.2-1.0 cm depending upon the vigour of the shoot. Scale leaves without, or with, only a faint resin gland.

Foliage is grey green in 'Haggerston Grey', grey blue in 'Naylor's Blue', dull bronzy yellow in 'Castlewellan' and with creamy white patches in 'Harlequin'.

Cones are rare on 'Haggerston Grey', but common on other forms, 1.5 cm in length; scales are shield-like, with a small spreading dorsal spine.

Evergreen tree

25-40 m

This is a hybrid of Nootka and Monterey cypresses. Although the two trees are both from western North America, they do not meet in the wild, and the hybrid has only occurred in the British Isles. It is closest to Nootka cypress. Its hybrid vigour or 'heterosis' is well known among gardeners and it grows much faster than either parent. As a result, it has replaced Monterey cypress as a hedging plant, to the fury of many a neighbour. It withstands trimming, and will grow 0.75-0.9 m a year; trimmed a couple of times a year, it creates a useful hedge or screen. However, there are better trees from which to form hedges, more forgiving if not trimmed regularly: these include yew, which is not much slower to make a neat hedge. *Cupressus leylandii* does not set seed and is propagated from cuttings. The most attractive form is 'Naylor's Blue', whose grey-blue foliage is especially pretty when the sun comes out after a shower.

'Castlewellan' is a seedling of the golden or 'Lutea' form of Monterey cypress but has rather dull bronze-coloured foliage. 'Harlequin' and 'Silver Dust' are two variegated forms of 'Haggerston Grey' fit for firewood.

Usually seen as a line or overgrown hedge, but can be attractive as a specimen free-standing tree. Shown here is the commonest form of Leyland cypress, the clone 'Haggerston Grey', which is the easiest to root from the cuttings.

BARK
Smooth and green-brown on young trees, on older trees becoming dark brown and developing shallow, stringy ridges.

Lawson cypress

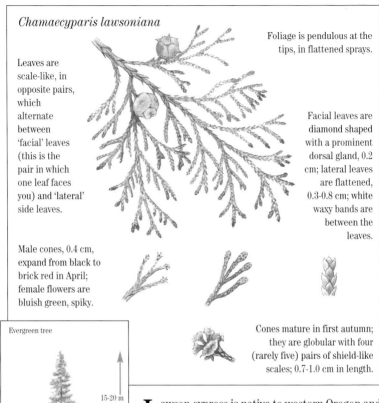

Chamaecyparis lawsoniana

Foliage is pendulous at the tips, in flattened sprays.

Leaves are scale-like, in opposite pairs, which alternate between 'facial' leaves (this is the pair in which one leaf faces you) and 'lateral' side leaves.

Facial leaves are diamond shaped with a prominent dorsal gland, 0.2 cm; lateral leaves are flattened, 0.3-0.8 cm; white waxy bands are between the leaves.

Male cones, 0.4 cm, expand from black to brick red in April; female flowers are bluish green, spiky.

Evergreen tree

15-20 m

Cones mature in first autumn; they are globular with four (rarely five) pairs of shield-like scales; 0.7-1.0 cm in length.

Lawson cypress is native to western Oregon and Northern California, where it forms large trees growing up to 50-60 m by 2 m, usually associated with species such as Douglas fir. The timber is light, soft and commercially useful. The tree is susceptible to root death caused by *Phytophthora*, single-celled yeast-like fungi which utilize the free sugars in the roots, thereby killing the tree. It is a waterborne disease and easily spread by wet soil on tyres. The disease is decimating the wild population and will kill trees in gardens, which are then available to be colonized by honey fungus, which, with its large fruit bodies and ability to digest wood, is then blamed for killing the tree.

The species was named after William Lawson, an Edinburgh nurseryman who first grew it. In its native Oregon it is called Port Orford cedar. Soon after it was introduced to Europe in 1850, it gave rise to cultivars and there are now several hundred named forms. I particularly like 'Intertexta', with its lax pendulous sprays of grey green foliage on erratically spreading branches.

Illustrated is a typical wild tree. Used as a specimen tree, as a screen or hedging, there are a large number of garden selections including tree forms; golden forms (such as *'Stewartii'*), blue forms (such as 'Pembury Blue'); and forms in which the juvenile pointed foliage persists (*'Ellwoodii'* and *'Fletcheri'*). There are also innumerable dwarf to slow-growing selections.

BARK
Shiny, smooth grey-green on young trees, becoming purple brown or red brown with fissures and fibrous ridges on old trees.

Sawara cypress

Chamaecyparis pisifera

Scale leaves are 0.15-0.4 cm long, mid green with pale waxy bands between the leaves on the underside; dorsal gland is not

Cone is globe shaped and angular, carried within the plane of the foliage, or slightly beneath it; 0.5-0.7 cm long. Four to six pairs of scales and a small spine.

Foliage is in flat and crowded sprays; leaves are scale-like, facial, and arranged in lateral similar pairs. Tips are acute and incurved but not pressed on to the shoot.

'Squarrosa' has only juvenile foliage, with soft needle-like leaves.

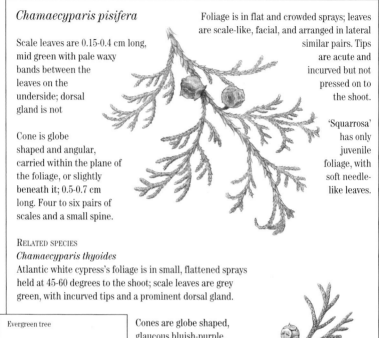

RELATED SPECIES
Chamaecyparis thyoides
Atlantic white cypress's foliage is in small, flattened sprays held at 45-60 degrees to the shoot; scale leaves are grey green, with incurved tips and a prominent dorsal gland.

Evergreen tree

15 m

Cones are globe shaped, glaucous bluish-purple, with three pairs of scales.

This cypress is native to the southern Japanese islands of Honshu and Kyushu, where it is one of the important timber trees because of its light, soft wood. In Europe, it is cultivated as an ornamental. The cultivar 'Aurea' is closest to the wild type, differing in the bright gold new foliage, which persists as yellow green. 'Plumosa' has partly juvenile foliage: the leaves are needle-like, but the free tips are only 0.2-0.4 cm, and yellowish grey green. 'Squarrosa' has fully juvenile bluish foliage, with the free tips to the leaves 0.5-0.7 cm long. 'Boulevard' is a form of 'Squarrosa' with much brighter foliage when growing well. Unfortunately, except on the very best moist sites, 'Boulevard' rarely grows well except in the nurseries. In most gardens it gets moth-eaten and tatty.

Atlantic white cypress comes from eastern USA from Maine to Georgia (but a related species occurs from Florida to Mississippi) growing on wetland sites. It makes a small tree, rarely more than 10 m high. In cultivation, it is mainly represented by three cultivars, 'Andelyensis', 'Glauca' and 'Variegata', whose foliage has large splashes of yellow.

26

Sawara cypress has given rise to a number of cultivars which are used as garden ornamentals, such as this fine example of the golden form, *Folifera Anrea*.

BARK
Reddish-brown or grey, initially smooth, but becoming deeply fissured with broad, slightly peeling ridges.

Incense cedar

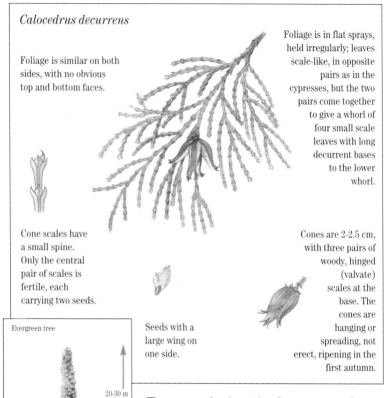

Calocedrus decurrens

Foliage is similar on both sides, with no obvious top and bottom faces.

Foliage is in flat sprays, held irregularly; leaves scale-like, in opposite pairs as in the cypresses, but the two pairs come together to give a whorl of four small scale leaves with long decurrent bases to the lower whorl.

Cone scales have a small spine. Only the central pair of scales is fertile, each carrying two seeds.

Cones are 2-2.5 cm, with three pairs of woody, hinged (valvate) scales at the base. The cones are hanging or spreading, not erect, ripening in the first autumn.

Evergreen tree

20-30 m

Seeds with a large wing on one side.

Incense cedar is native from western Oregon south to Baja California in northern Mexico and inland to western Nevada. Over this range, it has a broadly conical crown, with strong level branching, quite different from the usual narrow crowned form cultivated in Europe. Recently a remote population in northern Oregon to the east of Mount Hood has been found. It has much shorter branches and the crown is column shaped.

The common name derives from the fragrant and durable timber. It is soft, and can be worked with and across the grain, which makes it particularly useful pencils. Incense cedar is tolerant of a range of sites and conditions, and of honey fungus and *Phytophthora*, making it suitable for situations where these present a problem. The bark is usually thick and ridged, but some trees in the wild have attractive, flaky scaly bark. The cones show a relationship with *Thuja*, but the important differences between the two genera are that on *thuja* the cone has two to three pairs of fertile scales, the seeds have two equal wings and the cones are carried more or less erect on the foliage sprays.

In cultivation, these are trees with narrow crowns which tend to grow in a column shape.
Short, level branches predominate. Shown here is a specimen from the remote population in northern Oregon (see opposite) that was probably the source of those now seen in cultivation throughout Europe. It is growing in a forest of *Pinus ponderosa* (page 94).

BARK
Smooth grey and purple when young. Older trees become red brown and furrowed or scaly, with flaking scales.

Western red cedar

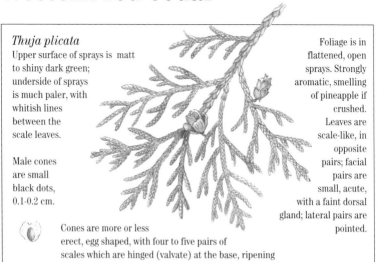

Thuja plicata

Upper surface of sprays is matt to shiny dark green; underside of sprays is much paler, with whitish lines between the scale leaves.

Male cones are small black dots, 0.1-0.2 cm.

Foliage is in flattened, open sprays. Strongly aromatic, smelling of pineapple if crushed. Leaves are scale-like, in opposite pairs; facial pairs are small, acute, with a faint dorsal gland; lateral pairs are pointed.

Cones are more or less erect, egg shaped, with four to five pairs of scales which are hinged (valvate) at the base, ripening in the first autumn. Scales come with a small hooked spine. Seeds are small, with two equal wings, and only carried on the middle two to three pairs of scales.

RELATED SPECIES
Thuja occidentalis
Eastern white cedar has foliage with a prominent dorsal gland and a sweet, apple-like aroma.

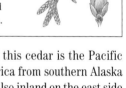

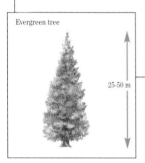

Evergreen tree

25-50 m

The natural range of this cedar is the Pacific coast of North America from southern Alaska to Northern California, also inland on the east side of the Rocky Mountains from interior British Columbia to northern Idaho. The wood is soft, easily worked, naturally durable, and familiar as the red-brown timber used for structures such as sheds or conservatories; also for roofing shingles and the cladding of modern bungalows. The Native Americans used it for canoes and totem poles. The common name derives from the red hue of the wood. In cultivation, the tree is used as an ornamental, and in forestry. It is a fast-growing tree and tolerates a wide range of sites, from dry sands, chalk and limestone to wet places.

Eastern white cedar is a much smaller and slower growing tree from eastern North America. An old name is 'Arbor vitae' or tree of life. This derives from the high vitamin C content of the foliage which was used by early explorers to prevent or cure scurvy. The cone is egg shaped, yellow-green to brown and the scales are smooth, without a dorsal prickle.

Western red cedar has an attractive crown which allows light to penetrate. This makes it useful for hedging: if the hedge needs to be reduced, there is usually live foliage to which it can be cut back.

BARK
Red brown and fissured, with narrow strips which often lift off; base of trunk is often fluted and expanded.

Hiba

Thujopsis dolobrata
Stout foliage is in flat sprays; upper surface is shiny mid green, underside has large white waxy patches.

Cones are more or less rounded, 1-2 cm, bluish green during the summer, but ripening brown in the first autumn; they have three to four pairs of thick, leathery hinged (valvate) scales, with an upturned prickle.

RELATED SPECIES
Platycladus orientalis
Biota or Chinese thuja's foliage is in flat sprays held erect; leaves are in rather similar pairs, without waxy bands.

Leaves are scale-like, in dissimilar opposite pairs, 0.4-1.0 cm; facial leaves are boat shaped, with a rounded free tip. Upper facial leaves have a faint resin gland, but no white waxy bands; however, underside has two white waxy bands. Lateral leaves are hatchet shaped, flattened with a free forward-pointing tip, and a large waxy band on the underside.

Cones egg - or grecian-urn shaped, erect, 1.5-2 cm Leathery scales, with a recurved spine. Seed 3 mm long, not winged.

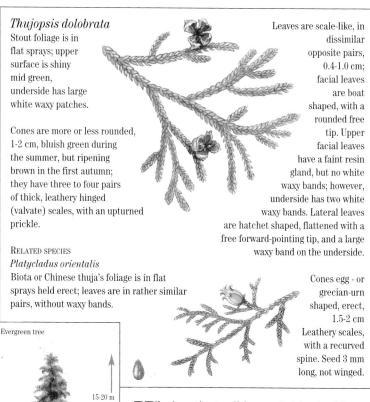

Evergreen tree

15-20 m

Hiba is native to all four main islands of Japan. The typical form occurs in the southern half of Honshu, Kyushu and Shikoku but in the northern part of Honshu and in Hokkaido it is replaced by var. *hondoensis* (which differs in its smaller and more densely packed scale leaves and the cone scales not having the upturned prickle). It produces a quality light timber, but grows too slowly in Britain and Europe to be used as a forestry tree. The generic name refers to its similarity to *Thuja* and the specific to the hatchet-shaped lateral leaves.

Platycladus orientalis is believed to be native to China from Beijing southwest to northern Yunnan, and may also be native to northern Iran; however, it is widely planted. It thrives in a range of climates, from the cold, dry winters and wet summers of Beijing, the changeable climate of Western Europe, to tropical Bangkok. It is often listed as a species of *Thuja,* but differs in having much larger cones, with leathery scales and large unwinged seeds; and in its foliage, which has rather similar facial and lateral leaves and is not scented. *Platycladus* will regenerate in the damp crumbling mortar of old walls.

Hiba makes an attractive, conical-shaped ornamental tree, often on several stems. As a member of the cypress family, its foliage typically grows to nearly ground level.

BARK
Brown and finely shredded, on older trees peeling in grey to purplish red-brown strips to reveal orange under bark.

Spanish juniper

Juniperus thurifera

Cone is 0.7-0.8 cm long, globe shaped with small prickles from vestigial scales, blue-green and waxy, ripening brown in second year. It contains two to four seeds.

Foliage is in short flat sprays, irregularly arranged around the shoot; leaves are scale-like, set in similar opposite pairs, decurrent on the shoot, 0.1-0.5 cm, apex triangular with a bony free tip. The dorsal resin gland is prominent and secretes white resin on older leaves.

SIMILAR SPECIES
Juniperus virginiana

Pencil cedar's foliage is mainly scale leaves in opposite pairs, but some paired juvenile leaves appear at the base and tips of the shoots. Scale leaves are 0.1-0.2 cm, grey green to dark green, with a small resin gland. Juvenile leaves are 0.3-0.6 cm long, needle-like, bloomed on the inner face. Cones (0.4-0.6 cm) are blue or brownish, with a thick waxy covering. They ripen in the first autumn and hold one to two seeds.

Juniperus chinensis

Chinese juniper's foliage is usually a mixture of scale leaves and needle-like juvenile leaves, broadly similar to pencil cedar's, but the juvenile leaves are in threes. Cones ripen over two years. Outlines of scales remain visible.

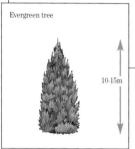

Evergreen tree

10-15m

Spanish juniper occurs throughout central, southern and eastern Spain, but is also found in south-eastern France in the Alps, and in North Africa. It is one of several juniper species found in the Mediterranean region which make small trees. Juniper cones are similar to those of cypresses, but the scales, instead of becoming woody, remains fleshy and the cone is like a berry. The original scales remain visible in some species, such as Spanish juniper and Chinese juniper, but not in others, such as pencil cedar.

Chinese juniper hails from most of China and coastal regions of Japan and is similarly used as an amenity tree, especially in the many cultivars (for example, 'Aurea', a male tree with yellow foliage, and 'Kaizuka', a female with predominantly adult foliage and laden with cones). The most useful characteristic, separating pencil cedar from Chinese juniper is that the juvenile leaves of pencil cedar are in pairs, in Chinese juniper threes. Cones are 0.5 cm long, expanding to 0.7-0.8 cm, egg shaped and dark brown by second winter, containing one to four shiny brown seeds.

Spanish juniper is characteristic of dry sites, where it occurs as scattered trees unless (such as along seasonal water courses) there is more moisture.

BARK
Dark brown and scaly, peeling in long strips on older trees.

Juniper

Juniperus

Fruit ripens over three summers, generally green in first year, waxy blue in second and ripening in third summer to blue black; it is egg shaped, 0.6-0.9 cm,

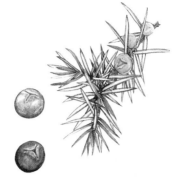

Foliage is in spreading, somewhat nodding three-dimensional sprays; leaves are 1-2 cm long, in whorls of threes, needle-like, tapering to a sharp bony point, prickly and jointed at the base but not decurrent on the greenish shoot.

RELATED SPECIES
Juniperus
Prickly juniper's leaves are 1-2.5 cm, needle-like, in whorls of three, softer and more lax in arrangement than in juniper, but also very sharp pointed.

Cones are egg shaped ripening in the second summer to dark reddish brown or violet purple, 0.5-1.0 cm, with usually

Evergreen tree, or a sprawling bush or prostrate shrub.

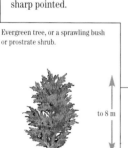

to 8 m

Juniper is the most widely distributed tree species, occurring throughout the northern temperate region, from Britain south to North Africa, east to Japan and in North America from much of Canada and south down both the Rocky Mountains and Appalachian Mountains. However, over most of this distribution it only makes a shrub, not a tree, and only occasionally exceeds 8 m in height. It tolerates a wide range of conditions, from chalks and limestones to acid peats, but requires moderate to full sunlight. The wood of juniper is only available in small quantities. When heated over a fire it produces a fragrant smoke which is used to smoke fish and other meats. The fruits are used to flavour the best gin.

Prickly juniper is native across southern Europe to the Caucasus, northern Iran and Iraq. It makes a larger tree than juniper, growing up to 15 m but also occuring as a sprawling shrub, usually on several stems. It is distinguished by the longer leaves, which have a grassy scent if crushed (as opposed to a sweet citrus scent in *J. communis*). The fruits ripen to brown in the second year.

Juniper occurs in many habit
forms, often in the same locality.
This specimen is typical – it is a
scrubby tree at the best of times.

BARK
Reddish-brown, on older
trees developing papery
scales.

Wellingtonia

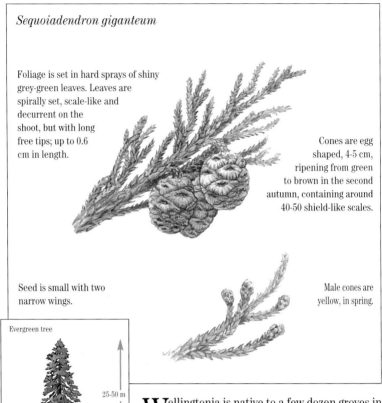

Sequoiadendron giganteum

Foliage is set in hard sprays of shiny grey-green leaves. Leaves are spirally set, scale-like and decurrent on the shoot, but with long free tips; up to 0.6 cm in length.

Cones are egg shaped, 4-5 cm, ripening from green to brown in the second autumn, containing around 40-50 shield-like scales.

Seed is small with two narrow wings.

Male cones are yellow, in spring.

Evergreen tree

25-50 m

Wellingtonia is native to a few dozen groves in the Sierra Nevada mountains of eastern California. The largest of all the trees has been named 'General Sherman': it has a bole diameter of 10 m, is 85 m in height and has been estimated to weigh 6,000 tons. Yet, like all of its kind, it grew from a seed weighing about 1/6,000 of a gramme. The bark may be 30 cm or more thick in old trees. It is soft and fibrous, but noticeably harder than the bark of *Sequoia*. Fibrous and easily excavated, it provides winter niches for treecreepers and other small birds. The timber is brittle and of low quality, not harvested.

The species first came to notice in 1854, after the death of the Duke of Wellington: a British botanist named it *Wellingtonia gigantea* in his honour. However, in a touch which would have pleased Napoleon, a Frenchman had earlier named an African genus after the Duke, so *Wellingtonia gigantea* could not stand as the botanical name. So it was placed in the genus *Sequoia*. There it stayed, long enough for the U.S. Congress to create the Sequoia National Park in order to preserve it. Later it was placed in a genus of its own.

In the wild, this forms impressive groves of enormous trees, but in Britain and Europe it is planted ornamentally as individual specimen trees as here, or in avenues. Other common names are big tree and Sierra redwood.

BARK
Red-brown and very thick, quickly developing deep ridges, often with small cup-shaped hollows caused by sheltering birds.

Coastal redwood

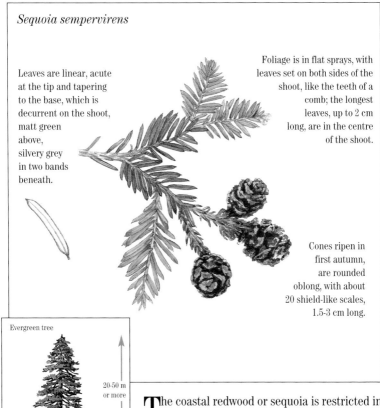

Sequoia sempervirens

Leaves are linear, acute at the tip and tapering to the base, which is decurrent on the shoot, matt green above, silvery grey in two bands beneath.

Foliage is in flat sprays, with leaves set on both sides of the shoot, like the teeth of a comb; the longest leaves, up to 2 cm long, are in the centre of the shoot.

Cones ripen in first autumn, are rounded oblong, with about 20 shield-like scales, 1.5-3 cm long.

Evergreen tree

20-50 m or more

The coastal redwood or sequoia is restricted in the wild to coastal California from just north of San Francisco into the south-western tip of Oregon: in other words, to the fog belt of the Californian coast and indeed, the tree is believed to receive a significant proportion of its water needs from intercepting fog. Quite how it manages to transport water and nutrients from the roots to the top of the tree is not known. The tallest tree is 114 m and a column of water this high would weigh more than 11 times atmospheric pressure. The very tallest trees are in valley bottoms where periodic flooding kills competing trees. The very thick bark is also a protection against forest fires. Coastal redwood's alternative names, sequoia, or redwood, differentiate it from *Sequoiadendron (*page 38). The generic name is after Sequoiah, son of a British trader and a Cherokee squaw, credited with inventing an alphabet for the Cherokee language. As both *Sequoiadendron* (page 38) and *Metasequoia* (page 42) are named for their affinity to *Sequoia*, Sequoiah has three tree genera named after him. Yet there is no evidence that he saw any of them.

Sequoia is one of the few conifers which produces coppice shoots at the base. The wood is excellent, used for sawn timber in house-building.

BARK
Red brown, extremely thick, with deep ridges, fibrous and very soft.

41

Dawn redwood

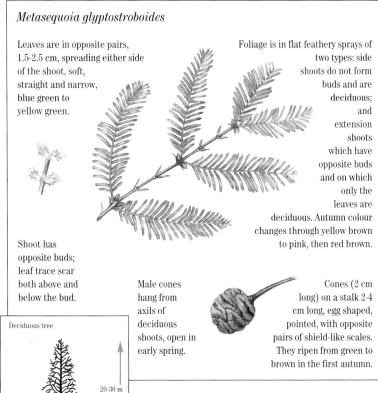

Metasequoia glyptostroboides

Leaves are in opposite pairs, 1.5-2.5 cm, spreading either side of the shoot, soft, straight and narrow, blue green to yellow green.

Foliage is in flat feathery sprays of two types: side shoots do not form buds and are deciduous; and extension shoots which have opposite buds and on which only the leaves are deciduous. Autumn colour changes through yellow brown to pink, then red brown.

Shoot has opposite buds; leaf trace scar both above and below the bud.

Deciduous tree

20-30 m

Male cones hang from axils of deciduous shoots, open in early spring.

Cones (2 cm long) on a stalk 2-4 cm long, egg shaped, pointed, with opposite pairs of shield-like scales. They ripen from green to brown in the first autumn.

Dawn redwood is native to a restricted area of Hubei and Sichuan provinces in central China. However, there are well-preserved specimens in the Canadian Arctic dated as 50 million years old, and fossils in coal from many places in the northern Hemisphere indicate that it was widespread. The surviving trees in China were only found in the 1940s and introduced to Europe in 1948. In the euphoria surrounding their discovery, the evocative name dawn redwood was given – and has stuck. The local Chinese name is water fir and this conjures up the boggy sites to which the tree has been restricted in the wild. However, whilst dawn redwood is happy to grow with its feet (and ankles) in water, it is happiest on a moist, deep soil and tolerate some dryish sites. This versatility has turned it into a popular amenity tree, greatly helped by the luxuriant foliage and attractive autumn colour. The shoots in winter are unique for the double scars around the buds. The buds are carried in a leaf axil and the scar beneath the bud is made when the leaf falls. The deciduous shoots are formed just above the buds and the upper scar is caused when they fall.

The feathery foliage on this tree's pleasing cone-shaped crown makes an attractive tree all year.

BARK
Orange-brown to red-brown, on young trees smooth, but soon developing papery scales, then fibrous with stringy ridges. Trunk is often fluted at the base.

Swamp cypress

Taxodium distichum

Leaves are 1-2 cm long, light green, turning brick red in November. Those on deciduous shoots fall on the shoot.

Foliage is in fern-like sprays of two forms: on the permanent shoots, the leaves are spirally set and scale-like; on deciduous shoots, the leaves are linear, lying flat on either side of the shoot.

Shoot has small, 0.1-0.15 cm, spirally-set buds. When grown on a waterlogged or very damp site, breathing roots are produced.

Cones are globe shaped, ripening from green to brown in first autumn, 2.5-3 cm, falling intact and usually breaking up on the ground to release the seeds; scales are shield-like.

SIMILAR SPECIES
Taxodium ascendens
Pond cypress's foliage is spirally set, bright green, up to 1 cm, initially in erect sprays.

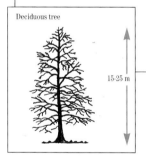

Deciduous tree

15-25 m

This is native to a broad sweep of south-eastern U.S.A. from New Jersey to Texas and up the Mississippi valley. It is characteristic of wet bottomland sites and thrives on periodic flooding. Although it can grow in permanent swamps, it is best suited to moist, well-drained sites; however, it cannot compete in such places with faster-growing broadleaved trees; whereas on flooded sites, its pneumatophores or 'knees' solve the problem of getting oxygen to the roots to allow them to respire. (Pneumatophores, illustrated in bark photo, are stubby structures which rise above soil level and allow the roots to breathe.)

Swamp cypress is also called bald cypress: it is deciduous in winter. Its native habitat is warmer than that of much of Europe, and normally it does not leaf until June; nor does the foliage change colour or drop until November.

Pond cypress is found in the wild from Virginia to Louisiana, but generally at low levels and around ponds rather than rivers. The leaves are scale-like on the deciduous shoots, and the tree very rarely produces knees. The botanical name refers to the ascending new foliage, but it droops by autumn.

Swamp cypress is well adapted to wet places, but is also perfectly happy on dry sites. Young trees are conical. Shown here is an old tree with a spreading crown.

BARK
Dull brown to reddish-brown, later fissured and, on older trees, peeling in narrow strips.

Japanese cedar

Cryptomeria japonica

Leaves are needle-like, soft and incurved, mid to dark green, with two whitish bands, up to 2 cm long, with the longest leaves in the middle part of the shoot.

Foliage is in three-dimensional sprays, set radially around the shoot in five rows.

Cones are globe shaped, ripening from green to brown in first autumn, with 20-30 scales. Scales are shield-like, with a dorsal recurved spine and three to five erect, triangular teeth.

Male cones develop in spring in the axils of leaves near the tips of last year's shoots. They are 0.4-0.8 cm long, egg shaped to oblong, and yellow green.

Evergreen tree

20-30 m

Japanese cedar is native to the southern part of the Japanese archipelago, but because it has been used in forestry throughout Japan for many centuries, its true native area is obscured by planting. Very stout old trees remain on the small southern Islet of Yakushima. It is one of the few conifers which will coppice, meaning regrow from the stump if cut down. It has a light, soft timber similar to that of the redwoods.

At least as common in cultivation is *elegans*. This is a fixed juvenile form in which the leaves are longer, more widely spaced and softer. It can make a tree up to 30 m high, but usually grows at an angle to the vertical. Cones are produced, but it is one of the easiest trees to root from cuttings. *Cryptomeria* also occurs in China south of the Yangtze River, where it is grown for its timber. Some treat this tree as a separate species, variety or form of Japanese cedar. It is marked out by its attractive, fresh, green, soft foliage, which tends to hang down more than the Japanese forms. However, it is not impossible that it was an early introduction from Japan.

Young trees are cone-shaped, but older ones have a rounded crown with spaced branches.

BARK
Red brown or orange-brown. Young trees exfoliate in small flakes; older trees have a thick, fibrous bark, which peels in long strips.

Yew

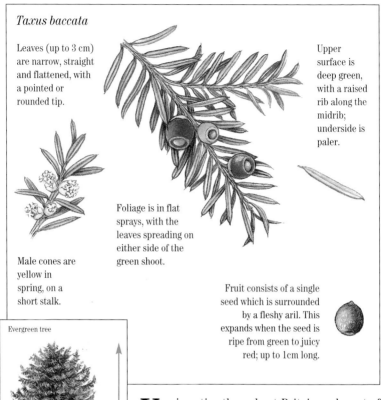

Taxus baccata

Leaves (up to 3 cm) are narrow, straight and flattened, with a pointed or rounded tip.

Upper surface is deep green, with a raised rib along the midrib; underside is paler.

Foliage is in flat sprays, with the leaves spreading on either side of the green shoot.

Male cones are yellow in spring, on a short stalk.

Fruit consists of a single seed which is surrounded by a fleshy aril. This expands when the seed is ripe from green to juicy red; up to 1cm long.

Evergreen tree

15-20 m

Yew is native throughout Britain and most of Europe, extending south into North Africa and east to Iran. It can make very stout trees, growing up to 2 m in diameter or more, but is usually less than 15 m in height. It is the longest lived of any European tree: specimens more than 2,000 years old are known. Yew has a reputation for being a slow grower but is capable of averaging 30 cm a year and will make a hedge nearly as quickly as Leyland cypress, (page 22). In fact, it is excellent for hedges, mazes and topiaries as it makes new growth if cut into leafless branches. Yew contains alkaloids which are poisonous to man and domestic beasts (but probably not to deer, seeing how readily they eat the foliage). Cattle and horses are killed by eating yew, as potentially are people, but the risk to humans is slight as the foliage is bitter. The only part of the tree not poisonous is the red aril: it contains sugars and is relished by badgers.

Yew has an excellent hard, dense timber. The old English longbow was made from yew, using lengths made up of the white sapwood for springiness and the dense heartwood for power.

Yew is usually seen as scattered trees (as here) but on chalk downs may form sombre, dense stands. These can be lightened in spring by the silvery new foliage of Whitebeams (page 188) growing alongside.

BARK
Smooth purplish-brown on young trees; on older ones, the bark develops scales which flake off to show red-brown, purple or yellow patches.

Larch

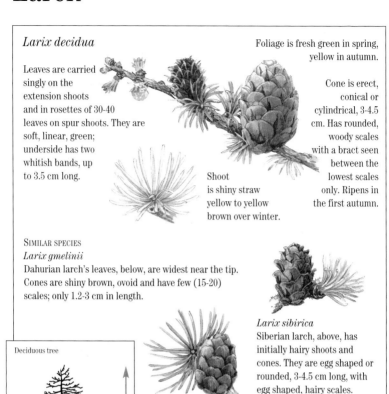

Larix decidua

Foliage is fresh green in spring, yellow in autumn.

Leaves are carried singly on the extension shoots and in rosettes of 30-40 leaves on spur shoots. They are soft, linear, green; underside has two whitish bands, up to 3.5 cm long.

Cone is erect, conical or cylindrical, 3-4.5 cm. Has rounded, woody scales with a bract seen between the lowest scales only. Ripens in the first autumn.

Shoot is shiny straw yellow to yellow brown over winter.

SIMILAR SPECIES
Larix gmelinii
Dahurian larch's leaves, below, are widest near the tip. Cones are shiny brown, ovoid and have few (15-20) scales; only 1.2-3 cm in length.

Larix sibirica
Siberian larch, above, has initially hairy shoots and cones. They are egg shaped or rounded, 3-4.5 cm long, with egg shaped, hairy scales.

Deciduous tree

20-40 m

Larch is native to Central Europe from the Alps north to the Tatra Mountains and east into the Carpathian Mountains. Its timber is durable, traditionally used in boat-building and fencing. The tree is planted both for timber and as a deciduous tree to break up plantations of evergreens. It also makes firebreaks: the foliage does not burn and there is no accumulation of flammable leaf litter. It leafs early in spring, turns bright yellow in late autumn and has strongly coloured shoots which give a yellow haze to a tree or forest: invaluable.

Siberian larch occurs from north-eastern Russia as far east into Siberia as Lake Baikal and south into the far west of China. It is best distinguished by the initially hairy shoots and the cone scales, which are egg-shaped to sub-rounded.

Dahurian larch is native to eastern Siberia east into north-eastern China. The smaller cones, with fewer scales, and the leaves, widest near the tip, are the most reliable identification features. In Britain and Western Europe Siberian and Dahurian larches come into leaf too early, often in January, and are damaged by spring frosts.

Larch forms dense forests in the Alps and Tatra Mountains, with scattered individuals at high levels. It is also widely planted as a forestry tree.

BARK
Smooth and grey in young trees, then red brown, developing fissures, and on old trees, coarsely ridged and scaly.

Japanese larch

Larix kaempferi
Foliage is bluish green or grey green, turning
pale yellow to orange in autumn, carried
singly on the extension shoots and in
rosettes of 20-35 leaves on spur
shoots. Leaves are soft,
linear, diamond
shaped in cross
section with hairs
at the base, up to 6
cm long but usually only 4 cm.

Shoot is reddish
purple, with a
waxy bloom in
the first winter.

Cone is erect, egg shaped, 2.5-3 cm, with reflexed, thin-but-stiff
woody scales; bracts not visible or only the cusp shows between the
scales; ripens in the first autumn to mid brown.

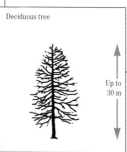

SIMILAR SPECIES
Larix marschlinsii
Hybrid larch has cones
intermediate between Japanese
larch and European larch.

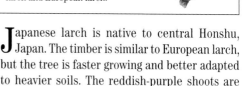

Deciduous tree

Up to
30 m

Japanese larch is native to central Honshu,
Japan. The timber is similar to European larch,
but the tree is faster growing and better adapted
to heavier soils. The reddish-purple shoots are
very different from the straw-yellow shoots of
European larch and give a plantation a purplish haze.

Hybrid or Dunkeld larch is a hybrid between Japanese and European larches. It is intermediate between the two species, and readily back crosses, thus
further masking the distinctions. Because the two parent species are closely
related, but have been separate for a long period, Dunkeld larch has hybrid
vigour or heterosis and grows fast in forestry plantations. The tree is also
known as *Larix eurolepis* (*L. europaea* being a synonym of European larch
and *L. leptolepis* being a synonym of Japanese larch).

The flowers of larches are carried on spur shoots at least two years old.
After flowering the spur shoots die. Sometimes a shoot will grow from the tip
of the cone but it only lasts one summer. The male flowers are yellow and the
female flowers often pink or purple.

Japanese larch brightens up early spring by flushing (coming into leaf) earlier than other trees. And it turns attractive colours in autumn.

BARK
Smooth and red or purplish-brown on young trees, becoming fissured and scaly in grey plates on old trees.

Cedar of Lebanon

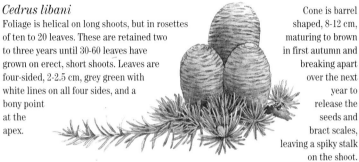

Cedrus libani

Foliage is helical on long shoots, but in rosettes of ten to 20 leaves. These are retained two to three years until 30-60 leaves have grown on erect, short shoots. Leaves are four-sided, 2-2.5 cm, grey green with white lines on all four sides, and a bony point at the apex.

Cone is barrel shaped, 8-12 cm, maturing to brown in first autumn and breaking apart over the next year to release the seeds and bract scales, leaving a spiky stalk on the shoot.

SIMILAR SPECIES

Cedrus atlantica

Atlas cedar's foliage is similar to that of Cedar of Lebanon, but has more leaves (30-45) in each year's growth on the short shoots. The leaves are 1.5-2.5 cm long and usually covered by wax, making the foliage blue or silvery.

Male cones in autumn end the short shoots. They are erect, up to 5 cm long, and produce masses of yellow pollen. Female flowers are cylindrical, green, 2 cm long, also ending the short shoots.

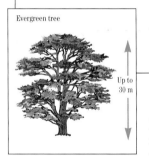

Evergreen tree

Up to 30 m

Cedar of Lebanon occurs wild in a small number of stands restricted to the western side of the Lebanon Mountains where they receive rainfall from the Mediterranean. It also occurs in north-western Syria and in southern Turkey, where the trees do not develop the typical broad, flat-topped crowns with foliage held horizontally. It has a fragrant and durable light timber which has been used over the millennia for building: witness the famous temple in Jerusalem which was ordered nearly three thousand years ago by King Solomon.

Atlas cedar is restricted to the Atlas Mountains of Morocco and Algeria, where it still forms forests. It is mainly cultivated as the blue foliage form, but, in the wild, trees with green foliage are also common. Both cedars will grow on a range of sites, but are especially tolerant of chalky soil. What they don't like is shade – they need full sunlight to look their best. Cedar of Lebanon was introduced in the 17th century but Atlas cedar arrived in the 1840s. Atlas cedar is nowadays much more widely planted and is more attractive as a young tree, but perhaps without the poise of a mature cedar of Lebanon.

Cedar of Lebanon develops horizontal flat-topped branches, as here, but young trees are spiky. The drawback to flat branches is their tendency to break under the weight of wet snow.

BARK
Dark grey or brown and smooth on young trees, becoming blackish and developing scaly ridges on old trees.

Deodar cedar

Cedrus deodara

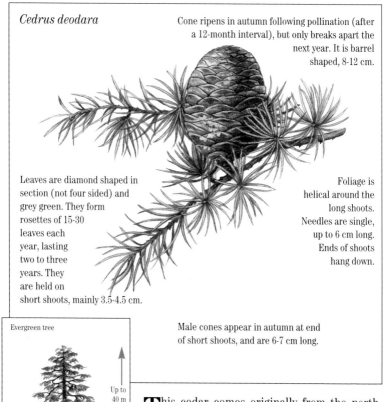

Cone ripens in autumn following pollination (after a 12-month interval), but only breaks apart the next year. It is barrel shaped, 8-12 cm.

Leaves are diamond shaped in section (not four sided) and grey green. They form rosettes of 15-30 leaves each year, lasting two to three years. They are held on short shoots, mainly 3.5-4.5 cm.

Foliage is helical around the long shoots. Needles are single, up to 6 cm long. Ends of shoots hang down.

Evergreen tree

Up to 40 m

Male cones appear in autumn at end of short shoots, and are 6-7 cm long.

This cedar comes originally from the north-western part of the Indian subcontinent, from western Nepal through to eastern Afghanistan. It makes an attractive amenity tree, but tends to look best as a young tree, when it grows vigorously, with a narrow crown and branch tips that hang down noticeably. Older trees only look good when they are growing on a moist site, otherwise they tend to become rather ragged, with dieback. It does not form the level, tiered branches characteristic of cedar of Lebanon. While cedar of Lebanon needs to be 50 years old to look its best, and Atlas cedar 15 to 20 years, deodars can be very attractive up to 20 years. Ideally, a replacement tree should be planted before the older tree is felled: but this is not the average gardener's idea of managing trees.

Deodar and *deodara* are derived from the Indian name for the species. Like the other cedars, it has a useful timber. In cultivation, all the true cedars (those which belong to the genus *Cedrus*) will hybridize, but deodar is the most distinctive one.

Deodar cedar makes an attractive ornamental tree, largely because of its hanging branches.

BARK
On young trees, smooth and grey, but this fissures to give wide black to pinkish-grey furrows and short scaly ridges.

Norway spruce

Picea abies

Leaves single, set on a projection of the shoot called a pulvinus, which is left behind when the needle falls but comes away if torn off.

Female cones at flowering time in spring are erect, only hanging down after pollination.

Foliage is parted beneath the shoot, with the side leaves spreading and those above the shoot pointing forwards.

Leaves are four-sided or quadrangular, up to 2.5 cm, linear but curved forwards, green to grey green. Set on a red brown, orange brown or golden brown shoot.

Cones cylindrical, 10-20 cm. They ripen to brown in autumn of first year, releasing the seeds over winter; scales rhombic, thin and woody.

SIMILAR SPECIES
Picea obovata
Siberian spruce has cylinder- or egg-shaped cones which are only 5-11 cm long and have rounded, moderately woody scales.

Evergreen tree

25-40 m

Norway spruce is found throughout Europe, but does not extend into Britain or Spain. Although the English common name refers to Norway, the best trees are perhaps from Central Europe. It is used as the principal Christmas tree species in Britain, but fortunately a wider range of species are becoming available for this purpose. It can be attractive when well grown, but almost any other spruce would be as good in the same conditions. Its white timber has a good quality and is used in building, for paper pulp and for the sounding boards of violins – in fact some call it violin wood. Widely planted as a forestry tree, it is, however, susceptible to drought and attacks by aphids. These suck the sap in the needles: in a severe attack, the needles are killed; when is less severe, bands across the middle of the needle are left pale yellowish.

Siberian spruce is native from northwestern Europe to central Siberia. It is not very closely related to Norway spruce, but where the two species have overlapped their ranges since the melting of the most recent ice age, they have formed a swarm of hybrids.

Norway spruce makes a neat and pleasing tree in mountain regions where it keeps its foliage down to ground level.

BARK
Red-brown and finely flaky in young trees, becoming scaly at the base and purple or grey in old trees.

Caucasian spruce

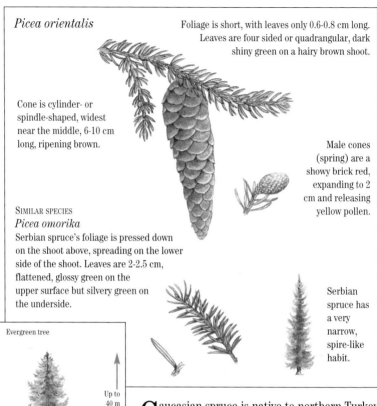

Picea orientalis

Foliage is short, with leaves only 0.6-0.8 cm long. Leaves are four sided or quadrangular, dark shiny green on a hairy brown shoot.

Cone is cylinder- or spindle-shaped, widest near the middle, 6-10 cm long, ripening brown.

Male cones (spring) are a showy brick red, expanding to 2 cm and releasing yellow pollen.

SIMILAR SPECIES
Picea omorika
Serbian spruce's foliage is pressed down on the shoot above, spreading on the lower side of the shoot. Leaves are 2-2.5 cm, flattened, glossy green on the upper surface but silvery green on the underside.

Serbian spruce has a very narrow, spire-like habit.

Evergreen tree

Up to 40 m

Caucasian spruce is native to northern Turkey along the Black Sea coast and to the Caucasus region. It makes a leafy tree, despite having the shortest needles of any spruce –it retains its needles for several years and has a neat habit. It is particularly attractive when the massed male cones are expanded in late spring, covering the top half of the tree with brick-red flowers giving off yellow pollen. The female flowers, in the upper part of the crown, are bright-red purple, more sparingly produced. The tree is grown in parks and gardens as a specimen or ornamental. It suffers from aphids less than Norway spruce.

Serbian spruce's native distribution is a few stands in the Drina River bordering Serbia and Bosnia-Herzegovina. It has small (3-6.5 cm) oval or-cone-shaped purplish-blue cones, usually restricted to the upper part of the tree. The narrow spire-like habit is very distinctive and believed to be an adaptation to prevent damage by wet snow. The side branches hang down, thereby restricting the spread of the tree. However, if the branches were held horizontally as in Norway spruce, the tree would be no narrower than that species.

Caucasian spruce makes an
attractive specimen tree. Mature
trees are column shaped, with
dense foliage. They often keep
their lower branches. Young trees
are spiky, and cone shaped with a
dense habit, usually retaining the
lower branches.

BARK
On young trees, pink-grey
and slightly roughened. On
older trees, it cracks into
rounded scales and
becomes brown or
sometimes grey brown.

Sitka spruce

Picea sitchensis

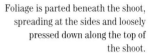

Leaves are linear, diamond-shaped in section, drawn out at the tip to a sharp bony point, 2-2.5 cm; upper surface is deep shiny green with no white bands or with two narrow white bands; underside has two grey-green or bluish bands.

Foliage is parted beneath the shoot, spreading at the sides and loosely pressed down along the top of the shoot.

Cones are cylindrical, ripening pale brown or whitish in first autumn, 5-10 cm; scales are thin, stiff with a jaggedly toothed margin.

SIMILAR SPECIES
Picea glauca
White spruce's foliage tends to be arranged more above the shoot than below; leaves curve forwards, are diamond-shaped in section, bluish green with white lines on all four sides, 1-1.7 cm.

White spruce's cones are long, egg-shaped, tapering to both ends, 2.5-6 cm; scales, are rounded, thin, woody and finely toothed.

Evergreen tree

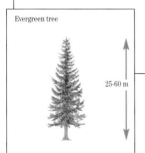

25-60 m

In its natural range, sitka spruce is found from Northern California up to Alaska along the Pacific coast of North America. It is a species of the coastal temperate rain forest belt and only found within 80 km of the sea. One of its American names is tideland spruce; the common name refers to Sitka in southern Alaska. The species likes, rather needs, plenty of rainfall and in the wild is not found on sites which dry out. It tolerates wind and exposure, although on shallow soils it is likely to be uprooted by strong winds. The timber is strong and useful, both for sawlogs and for pulp, and the tree is planted by the million in forestry. The foliage is susceptible to sap-sucking aphids, especially on dry sites, and these will lead to unhealthy trees, lacking vigour. This is one of the western North American trees to have reached 60 m this side of the Atlantic and can form large, majestic trees in little more than a century. In Canada it has exceeded 90 m.

White spruce occurs from inland Alaska across to the Atlantic seaboard of Canada. It is smaller and slower growing than Sitka spruce.

Sitka spruce is attractive as an indivdual tree, as here, showing the silvery undersides. But these are not so noticeable when planted in vast numbers, as it often is. Fast growth on poor soils, and quality timber, make it the first-choice commercial forestry tree in wet upland areas of Britain and Denmark.

BARK
Purplish-brown on young trees, becoming greyer on old trees and developing scales which flake off in concave plates, especially in the lower trunk.

Colorado blue spruce

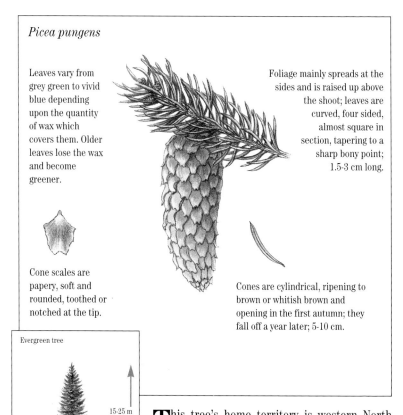

Picea pungens

Leaves vary from grey green to vivid blue depending upon the quantity of wax which covers them. Older leaves lose the wax and become greener.

Foliage mainly spreads at the sides and is raised up above the shoot; leaves are curved, four sided, almost square in section, tapering to a sharp bony point; 1.5-3 cm long.

Cone scales are papery, soft and rounded, toothed or notched at the tip.

Cones are cylindrical, ripening to brown or whitish brown and opening in the first autumn; they fall off a year later; 5-10 cm.

Evergreen tree

15-25 m

This tree's home territory is western North America from Wyoming and Idaho south to New Mexico, Arizona and Colorado. This is a relatively dry part of the continent and the tree is restricted either to small stands along streams, or to north-facing slopes where evaporation is least. Both green- and blue-foliaged forms occur in the wild, but it is the bluest forms which have been selected by nurserymen and make the overwhelming majority of trees sold in Britain and Europe. At their best, the blue forms can be quite impressive, especially as young trees, but they tend to suffer in several ways. The tree needs plenty of moisture to grow really well, but often fails to get enough because towns are generally in drier parts. The foliage loses its attractive waxy layer as it ages, and becomes green. Worse, the species is susceptible to defoliation by aphids; and finally, the older shoots are brown, so when they have lost their leaves they make an ugly contrast to blue foliage. There are better spruces for the discerning gardener. Grabbing hold of the foliage can also be painful: there are sharp,bony points in the stout needles.

Colorado blue spruce is primarily planted in gardens and parks in one of its blue selections. These are raised as grafted plants and need training when young to make an erect tree.

BARK
Red-brown or purple-grey, developing scaly plates which flake off.

Brewer's spruce

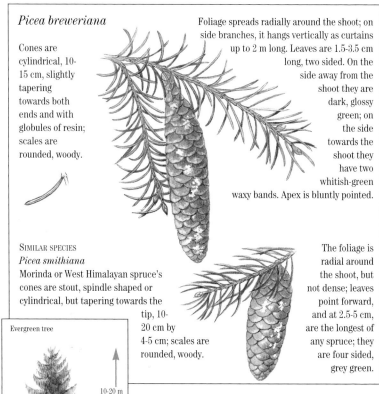

Picea breweriana

Cones are cylindrical, 10-15 cm, slightly tapering towards both ends and with globules of resin; scales are rounded, woody.

Foliage spreads radially around the shoot; on side branches, it hangs vertically as curtains up to 2 m long. Leaves are 1.5-3.5 cm long, two sided. On the side away from the shoot they are dark, glossy green; on the side towards the shoot they have two whitish-green waxy bands. Apex is bluntly pointed.

SIMILAR SPECIES
Picea smithiana
Morinda or West Himalayan spruce's cones are stout, spindle shaped or cylindrical, but tapering towards the tip, 10-20 cm by 4-5 cm; scales are rounded, woody.

The foliage is radial around the shoot, but not dense; leaves point forward, and at 2.5-5 cm, are the longest of any spruce; they are four sided, grey green.

Evergreen tree

10-20 m

Brewer's spruce is restricted in the wild to the Siskiyou Mountains of south-western Oregon and Northern California in a region which escaped being glaciated in the most recent Ice Age. It occurs with pines, silver firs and Douglas fir. It can grow beyond 50 m with a 1 m bole diameter. Its curtains of hanging foliage and the smooth, scaly bark are impressive.

In cultivation, Brewer's spruce has not made such large trees, but then it was only introduced in 1897. Give it another 400 years, and who knows what it will make. The tree thrives in drier parts of Britain. Young trees are very slow to adopt the adult weeping foliage, partly because the young foliage is much finer, but also because hanging foliage requires the stem to make height and then develop side branches before the shoots can droop.

Morinda or West Himalayan spruce is superficially similar in the hanging side shoots, and also makes an attractive tree. However, it is not related to Brewer's spruce: its foliage is four sided, more lax on the shoot and green; the cones are much bulkier. It is a native of West Himalaya, prefering moist sites.

The cylindrical crown is curtained by the hanging side shoots and gives the tree its graceful habit.

Smooth and grey on young trees, developing scaly plates which flake off to reveal brown or purple bark, but remaining rather smooth.

Douglas fir

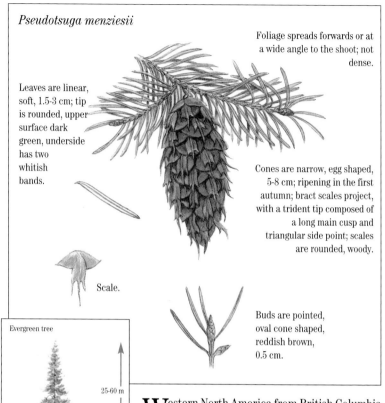

Pseudotsuga menziesii

Foliage spreads forwards or at a wide angle to the shoot; not dense.

Leaves are linear, soft, 1.5-3 cm; tip is rounded, upper surface dark green, underside has two whitish bands.

Cones are narrow, egg shaped, 5-8 cm; ripening in the first autumn; bract scales project, with a trident tip composed of a long main cusp and triangular side point; scales are rounded, woody.

Scale.

Buds are pointed, oval cone shaped, reddish brown, 0.5 cm.

Evergreen tree

25-60 m

Western North America from British Columbia through the U.S.A. into central Mexico is the natural range of this species. Covering such a vast area it shows considerable variation and is usually divided into two subspecies. The typical form, with green foliage and corky bark, is found in northern and coastal parts on the western side of the Rocky Mountains. It grows up to 90 m and up to 3 m in diameter. It is a fire-dominant species, regenerating after forest fires and then surviving future ones because of the thick bark. In the absence of fire, it eventually dies and is replaced by shade tolerant species, such as grand fir *Abies grandis* (page 74).

Blue Douglas fir, (subspecies *glauca*), has leaves with a waxy blue covering on the upper surface: a device for restricting water loss. It also has generally smaller and narrower cones with bracts that spread more, and dark grey or blackish, scaly bark, which does not develop the high corky ridges of the green form. It occurs in drier zones on the eastern side of the Rocky Mountains, where it makes a much smaller tree.

Douglas fir makes a majestic tree, used in forestry for its high-quality timber.

BARK
Grey green and smooth, with blisters of resin on young trees, becoming thick and corky with proud ridges and wide furrows. Reddish brown or grey brown on old trees.

European silver fir

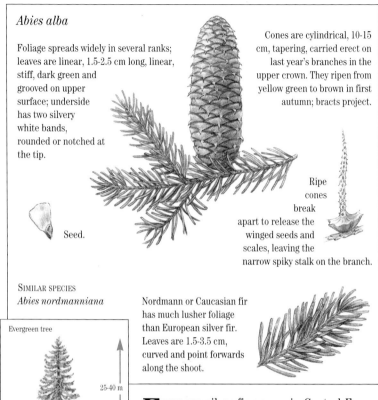

Abies alba

Foliage spreads widely in several ranks; leaves are linear, 1.5-2.5 cm long, linear, stiff, dark green and grooved on upper surface; underside has two silvery white bands, rounded or notched at the tip.

Cones are cylindrical, 10-15 cm, tapering, carried erect on last year's branches in the upper crown. They ripen from yellow green to brown in first autumn; bracts project.

Ripe cones break apart to release the winged seeds and scales, leaving the narrow spiky stalk on the branch.

Seed.

SIMILAR SPECIES
Abies nordmanniana

Nordmann or Caucasian fir has much lusher foliage than European silver fir. Leaves are 1.5-3.5 cm, curved and point forwards along the shoot.

Evergreen tree

25-40 m

European silver fir occurs in Central Europe from southern Germany through the Alps to the Carpathian Mountains and south into the Balkans, Italy, eastern France and Spain (in the Pyrenees). It likes better-quality sites with deeper and richer soils, and often forms forests mixed with beech. The timber is of high quality, pale yellowish and odourless, which makes it suitable for butter boxes and the like. Silver fir is the traditional European Christmas tree which was introduced into Britain by Prince Albert in the 1840s. It was soon supplanted by the much less suitable Norway spruce (which drops its needles): an aphid restricted the growing of silver fir in Britain.

Nordmann or Caucasian fir makes an impressive tree, with its dense and luxuriant foliage and ability to grow on drier sites. It occurs in the wild in north-eastern Turkey and in the western Caucasus from Georgia and Abkhazia. It has gained popularity as a Christmas tree, partly for the dense habit, but especially because the needles do not fall when brought inside. The leaves are retained for four to six years but occasionally for up to 25 years.

Silver fir is a tree of the lower
slopes of mountain forests, where
it is often associated with beech.
Mature trees have a column shape
and often show silvery bark on the
lower trunk.

BARK
Grey brown or grey,
smooth on young trees,
but becoming cracked into
small scaly plates on old
trees.

Greek fir

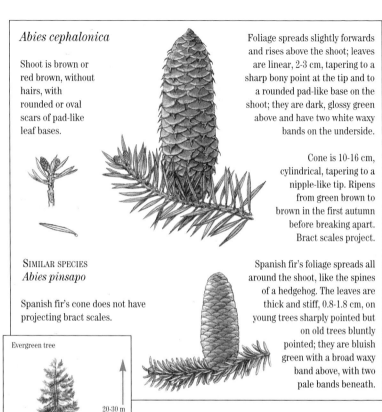

Abies cephalonica

Shoot is brown or red brown, without hairs, with rounded or oval scars of pad-like leaf bases.

Foliage spreads slightly forwards and rises above the shoot; leaves are linear, 2-3 cm, tapering to a sharp bony point at the tip and to a rounded pad-like base on the shoot; they are dark, glossy green above and have two white waxy bands on the underside.

Cone is 10-16 cm, cylindrical, tapering to a nipple-like tip. Ripens from green brown to brown in the first autumn before breaking apart. Bract scales project.

SIMILAR SPECIES
Abies pinsapo

Spanish fir's cone does not have projecting bract scales.

Spanish fir's foliage spreads all around the shoot, like the spines of a hedgehog. The leaves are thick and stiff, 0.8-1.8 cm, on young trees sharply pointed but on old trees bluntly pointed; they are bluish green with a broad waxy band above, with two pale bands beneath.

Evergreen tree

20-30 m

As the Latin name indicates, Greek fir was first named after Cephalonia, an island off the west coast of Greece. It is also found throughout most of the Greek mainland; further to the north it shows characteristics of *Abies alba* (page 70). In northern Greece and the southern Balkans there is an intermediate species (*A. borisii-regis*). Greek fir is planted in parks and gardens and can grow to a massive size. It may get damaged by late spring frosts, but is well adapted to hot, dry climates. The pad-like bases to the leaves are characteristic.

Spanish fir is restricted in the wild to three forests around Ronda in southern Spain, but will grow throughout most of Europe. It is distinguished by the short, thick leaves held in a very nearly perfectly radial arrangement with leaves of similar length (in other species, they are of differing lengths on the same shoot). They are responsible for the alternative common name of hedgehog fir. In young trees, the needles are sharp and pointed, unlike the blunt adult foliage. The bark is dark grey and smooth, fissuring on old trees. Spanish fir thrives on all soil types, but is especially adapted to dry and chalky sites.

Mature trees of Greek fir develop a stout bole with a few large spreading branches, which may make secondary leaders. Young trees tend to be cone shaped, with branches in spaced whorls.

BARK
Smooth, finely flaky and grey, with a tinge of pink or brown on young trees, fissuring into small scaly plates on old trees.

Grand fir

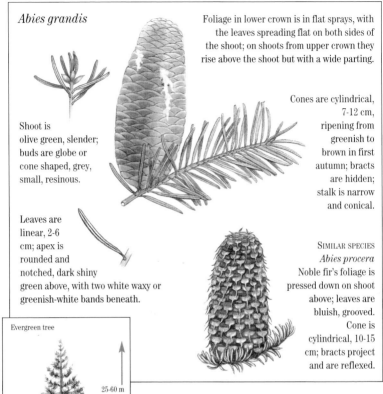

Abies grandis

Foliage in lower crown is in flat sprays, with the leaves spreading flat on both sides of the shoot; on shoots from upper crown they rise above the shoot but with a wide parting.

Shoot is olive green, slender; buds are globe or cone shaped, grey, small, resinous.

Leaves are linear, 2-6 cm; apex is rounded and notched, dark shiny green above, with two white waxy or greenish-white bands beneath.

Cones are cylindrical, 7-12 cm, ripening from greenish to brown in first autumn; bracts are hidden; stalk is narrow and conical.

SIMILAR SPECIES
Abies procera
Noble fir's foliage is pressed down on shoot above; leaves are bluish, grooved. Cone is cylindrical, 10-15 cm; bracts project and are reflexed.

Evergreen tree

25-60 m

Grand fir's native range is from Northern California north to Vancouver Island along the west coast of America and inland into southeastern British Columbia and northern Idaho. It has a rather low-quality timber, partly because it grows so fast. The fastest growing specimens originate from the coastal ranges west of the Cascade Mountains of Oregon and Washington; those originating from east of the Cascades and from Idaho are much slower growing.

In most European gardens, it makes the tallest tree after a hundred years, emerging 10 m or more above the heads of other trees and suffering from exposure to the wind. It is at its best in sheltered moist sites, where it will retain its foliage down to ground level and can be very attractive.

Noble fir also comes from Oregon and Washington states of the Pacific U.S.A. It has a better-quality timber, although in cultivation may form 'drought' cracks in dry years, which show as roughly metre-long on the smooth, shiny, silvery-grey bark in the upper part of the trunk. Large cones are produced on young trees. It needs acidic sites, and will not tolerate chalky soils.

Grand fir is often the tallest tree in its vicinity when it becomes ragged from exposure. But in sheltered sites it retains its foliage down to ground level, as here.

BARK
Smooth, with blisters of resin Brownish grey on young trees, on old trees cracking into small squares.

White fir

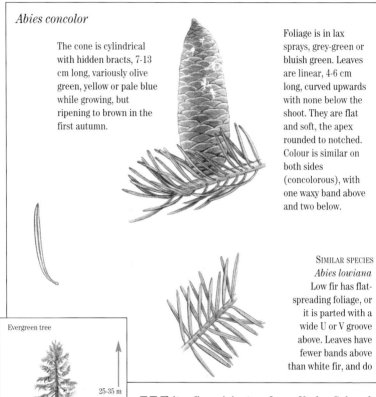

Abies concolor

The cone is cylindrical with hidden bracts, 7-13 cm long, variously olive green, yellow or pale blue while growing, but ripening to brown in the first autumn.

Foliage is in lax sprays, grey-green or bluish green. Leaves are linear, 4-6 cm long, curved upwards with none below the shoot. They are flat and soft, the apex rounded to notched. Colour is similar on both sides (concolorous), with one waxy band above and two below.

SIMILAR SPECIES
Abies lowiana
Low fir has flat-spreading foliage, or it is parted with a wide U or V groove above. Leaves have fewer bands above than white fir, and do

Evergreen tree

25-35 m

White fir originates from Utah, Colorado, Nevada, Arizona, California and New Mexico in south-western U.S.A. and extends into northern Mexico. It is characterized by sparse foliage which has a waxy bloom on the upper surface of the leaf. In the wild it is an invasive species, regenerating into the stands of other trees. But it cannnot tolerate fierce forest fires. In cultivation in Britain and Europe it tolerates drier conditions than the related grand fir, but has no role in forestry. It is sometimes planted as a Christmas tree but mainly it is a park or garden tree, valued for its bright blue foliage.

Low fir is often treated as a variety of white fir. It comes from the Sierra Nevada of California, also Northern California and south-west Oregon. In cultivation it makes a better tree than white fir, although the foliage is never so blue. The leaves are similarly spaced or lax on the shoot, but the arrangement is much flatter, with fewer lines of stomata or breathing pores. This may be the result of hybridization between white fir and grand fir, and in several respects is intermediate between them.

White fir makes an attractive tree within its bloomed or greyish foliage and will tolerate drier conditions than grand fir.

BARK
Smooth, light to dark grey, with resin blisters on young trees. Thick corky furrows and ridges on old trees.

Korean fir

Abies koreana
Leaves are 1-2 cm long and slightly broader towards the rounded notched apex. Upper surface is dark, shiny green; underside has two broad, vivid silver waxy bands.

Mature cones are cylindrical, with a nipple-like tip, 5-7 cm long, ripening from purple or greenish purple to light brown in the first autumn. Bracts project.

Foliage is spaced and arranged somewhat radially around the shoot, although with fewer leaves on the underside.

Young cones develop in late spring, ranging from purple, red or greenish yellow.

SIMILAR SPECIES
Abies veitchii
The foliage of Veitch's silver fir is parted beneath the shoot and somewhat above; leaves are longer than that of Korean fir, 2-2.5 cm; apex is rounded squarish with a notch; they have a waxy bloom above and two vivid silver bands beneath.

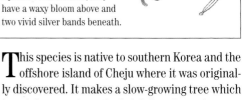

Evergreen tree

10-15 m

This species is native to southern Korea and the offshore island of Cheju where it was originally discovered. It makes a slow-growing tree which is quick to produce the brightly coloured cones. However, on some trees the cones are greenish, not violet purple, and much inferior. The foliage is always good, with dramatically silvered undersides. It tolerates a range of sites and its limited stature, makes it a useful tree for small gardens. Some of the populations from mainland Korea may, however, grow into larger trees than the Cheju island plants.

Veitch's silver fir comes from central Honshu. It was first discovered on Mount Fuji by John Veitch in 1860 and introduced to Europe soon after. Closely related to Korean fir, it differs primarily in the foliage. This is arranged above the shoot and points forwards. The leaves are much longer and narrower than that of Korean fir and are distinctly squarish at the apex; they have a waxy bloom on the upper surface. The underside is silvery. It does, however, make a much larger and faster-growing tree, so it is more suited to large gardens. It also tolerates a range of soils, but is not long lived in cultivation.

This small growing tree is widely planted as an ornamental for the attractive cones.

BARK
Smooth and grey with a purple or orange tinge. Resin blisters can be found on young trees. It matures and fissures into grey-black squares at the base of older trees.

Western hemlock

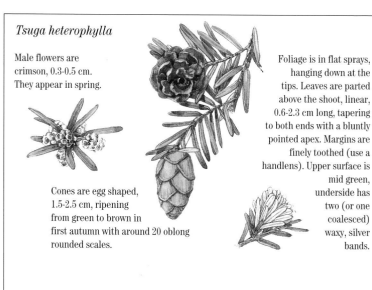

Tsuga heterophylla

Male flowers are crimson, 0.3-0.5 cm. They appear in spring.

Cones are egg shaped, 1.5-2.5 cm, ripening from green to brown in first autumn with around 20 oblong rounded scales.

Foliage is in flat sprays, hanging down at the tips. Leaves are parted above the shoot, linear, 0.6-2.3 cm long, tapering to both ends with a bluntly pointed apex. Margins are finely toothed (use a handlens). Upper surface is mid green, underside has two (or one coalesced) waxy, silver bands.

SIMILAR SPECIES
Tsuga canadensis
Eastern hemlock's foliage always has a line of short leaves lying along the top of the shoot. These show white undersides.

Evergreen tree

25-40 m

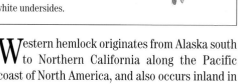

Western hemlock originates from Alaska south to Northern California along the Pacific coast of North America, and also occurs inland in south-eastern British Columbia and northern Idaho. It makes a most graceful tree, with dense, green, soft foliage carried on slender shoots hanging down noticeably at the tips. It acquired its common name from the foliage, which has a parsley or hemlock-like scent when crushed. However, it is not poisonous like the true hemlock (which is a herb in the *Umbelliferae* or carrot family). The inner bark is red and has been used to make a form of bread. Western hemlock tolerates a wide range of sites, but particularly likes dry acidic sands. It has an excellent timber, is fast growing, tolerant of shade, but likes shelter. Unfortunately, it is susceptible to a fungus, *Fomes* or *Heterobasidion annosum,* which rots the butt section of the trunk. This limits its use in forestry.

Eastern hemlock originates in eastern U.S.A. from New England south to Alabama and west to Ontario. It is very similar to western hemlock, but can is distinguished by the line of short upturned leaves along the shoot.

Graceful in habit and tolerant of dense shade, western hemlock makes an attractive tree.

BARK
Smooth and purple brown on young trees, becoming red brown or grey brown and developing furrows and scaly ridges.

Scots pine

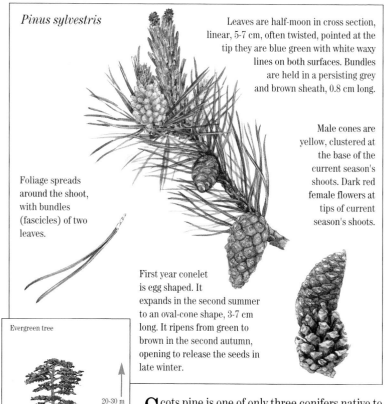

Pinus sylvestris

Leaves are half-moon in cross section, linear, 5-7 cm, often twisted, pointed at the tip they are blue green with white waxy lines on both surfaces. Bundles are held in a persisting grey and brown sheath, 0.8 cm long.

Male cones are yellow, clustered at the base of the current season's shoots. Dark red female flowers at tips of current season's shoots.

Foliage spreads around the shoot, with bundles (fascicles) of two leaves.

First year conelet is egg shaped. It expands in the second summer to an oval-cone shape, 3-7 cm long. It ripens from green to brown in the second autumn, opening to release the seeds in late winter.

Evergreen tree

20-30 m

Scots pine is one of only three conifers native to the British Isles. It has a very wide distribution, from Scotland in the west, south to Spain and Turkey, north into the Arctic and east as far as eastern China, differing little over this vast swathe of Eurasia. The timber is high quality, known as red deal or yellow deal (the heartwood is reddish, while the outer sapwood is yellow). It is used mainly for sawlogs, but also for veneers and telegraph poles – the modern equivalent of its use for masts and spars of sailing ships in earlier times. Along with birch, Scots pine was the first tree to recolonize the land left bare as the ice retreated after the most recent ice age. It will seed into poor sandy soils, where it can outgrow other trees, but on richer soils it cannot compete with faster-growing broadleaves. In England it had disappeared by the Middle Ages, partly as it was outgrown on most soils; on heaths and the like it was probably killed by felling and burning for grazing. The bundles or fascicles of pine tree leaves are actually short shoots. If put together they form a perfect cylinder, whether the tree has two, three or five leaves per fascicle.

Scots pine makes an attractive tree, with its blue-green foliage and two-coloured trunk. It is common in forestry, but also commonly planted in parks and gardens. Young trees are conical (as here). Older trees are rounded and domed.

BARK
On young trees and upper trunk of old trees, red brown or orange brown and flaky, abruptly changing to the mature bark, which is purple grey, fissured with purple-grey ridges shedding small thick scales.

Lodgepole pine or shore pine

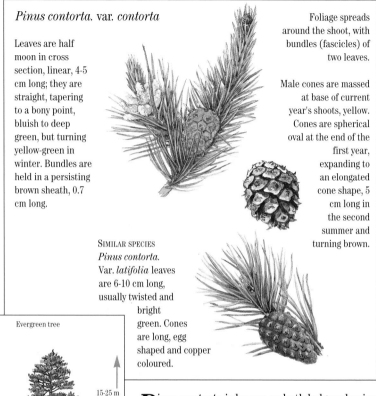

Pinus contorta. var. *contorta*

Leaves are half moon in cross section, linear, 4-5 cm long; they are straight, tapering to a bony point, bluish to deep green, but turning yellow-green in winter. Bundles are held in a persisting brown sheath, 0.7 cm long.

Foliage spreads around the shoot, with bundles (fascicles) of two leaves.

Male cones are massed at base of current year's shoots, yellow. Cones are spherical oval at the end of the first year, expanding to an elongated cone shape, 5 cm long in the second summer and turning brown.

SIMILAR SPECIES
Pinus contorta.
Var. *latifolia* leaves are 6-10 cm long, usually twisted and bright green. Cones are long, egg shaped and copper coloured.

Evergreen tree

15-25 m

*P**inus contorta* is known as both lodgepole pine and shore pine. Shore pine (var. *contorta*) is the form from the Pacific coast of North America from Alaska to Northern California, always within 160 km of the coast, and frequently on sand dunes just out of reach of the sea. In exposed sites it may only form a shrub, but given better soil and a little shelter, it will make an upright tree, with respectable, if not fast, growth. The timber is satisfactory rather than good; it quickly degrades on windblown trees. It has been used for forestry over large areas of upland Britain and Ireland and also in parts of Scandinavia, and is tolerant of very poor site conditions and exposure. The long shoots can make either a single node or several nodes: look for the cones which are at the tips of the nodes, and the male cones (or the bare patch they leave) at the base of the shoot above the node. The cones persist on the tree, opening on maturity.

Lodgepole pine (var. *latifolia*) is the form which occurs along the Rocky Mountain chain from the Yukon to Colorado. The foliage is longer, and twisted. Most of the cones do not open on ripening: it takes a forest fire to do this.

Pinus contorta can make a large tree when old, with a domed crown, but is more commonly seen in forestry plantings, where the trees are harvested while still with a spiky crown. This photograph shows an example of lodgepole pine intermediate between the two forms. Native Americans used the timber as tent supports.

BARK
Red-brown or yellow-brown on young trees, developing deep fissures and dark scales or plates on old trees.

European black pine

Pinus nigra

Leaves are half moon in cross section, linear, 8-14 cm long, sharply pointed at the tip, and stiff; they are grey green, with silvery lines of dots on both surfaces; bundles are held in a persisting dark brown sheath, 1-1.3 cm long.

Foliage spreads around the shoot, with bundles (fascicles) of two leaves.

Cones open over winter and falls in the third spring. Cone scales have a blunt ridge.

First-year cone is egg shaped, 1.3 cm long, expanding in the second year to an oval cone shape and ripening yellow brown or brown.

Evergreen tree

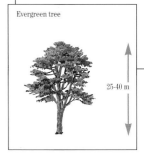

25-40 m

European black pine is a native of Europe from France and Spain to Turkey, Cyprus and the Ukraine; it is also seen in Morocco and Algeria. It can be divided into two subspecies: ssp. *nigra* includes the trees from southern Austria and central Italy eastwards. This form tends to have denser foliage in more pronounced annual growths. The trees often have several stems, giving characteristic mature habits, and are not much use in forestry. The second subspecies is ssp. *salzmannii* which differs in the longer (12-18 cm), thinner foliage. This form occurs from the Alps into Spain and North Africa, and includes Corsican pine (var. *corsicana*; synonym var. *maritima*) which is found in Corsica, Calabria and Sicily. Corsican pine is widely used in British forestry for its fast growth on poor sandy soils, but it will also tolerate chalk and limestone soils. It has a reasonable softwood timber, used for sawlogs. It needs full sun for best development, and is well adapted to the harsh Mediterranean climate. Young seedlings must make an extensive root system as soon as they germinate if they are not to be burnt off by summer drought.

Dense, grey-green foliage on spreading branches gives European black pine a distinctive appearance. This is a sypical mature ssp. *nigra*.

BARK
Dark brown or greenish-black on young trees, initially smooth, but soon developing deep fissures with broad, scaly ridges.

Maritime pine

Pinus pinaster

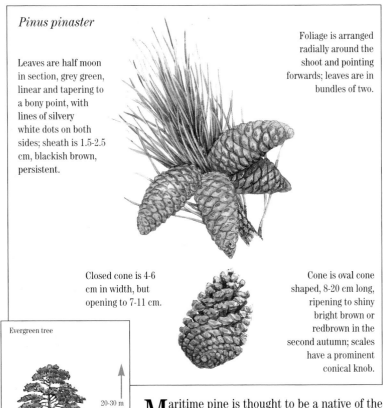

Leaves are half moon in section, grey green, linear and tapering to a bony point, with lines of silvery white dots on both sides; sheath is 1.5-2.5 cm, blackish brown, persistent.

Foliage is arranged radially around the shoot and pointing forwards; leaves are in bundles of two.

Closed cone is 4-6 cm in width, but opening to 7-11 cm.

Cone is oval cone shaped, 8-20 cm long, ripening to shiny bright brown or redbrown in the second autumn; scales have a prominent conical knob.

Evergreen tree

20-30 m

Maritime pine is thought to be a native of the northern sides of the Mediterranean region from Portugal east to Greece and on the southern shore in Morocco. There are also extensive forests in the Les Landes district of south-western France, but these were planted in the 19th century and the species is almost certainly not native to this part of the country. It is mainly a tree of coastal sand dunes, hence maritime pine, but in Morocco occurs in the mountains up to 2000 m. Maritime pine is also called cluster pine, as the cones are often carried in large clusters, as opposed one to three in other pine species. The timber is of moderate quality: however, its principal product is the resin, quaintly known as 'naval stores' from its earlier use. The resin is extracted by cutting V grooves in through the bark and collected in small bowls. It is refined to give turpentine and rosin, which is used on the strings of violins and other instruments and also to 'size' (fill) some grades of paper. This is a serotinous pine, a term applied to the pine species which keep the cones closed until they are opened by a forest fire.

Maritime pine makes a medium-sized tree with an open crown. Mature trees have a rounded crown set high on a naked stem. They usually lose their lower branches.

BARK
Orange brown and fissured on young trees,, but developing deep rust-brown fissures and narrow dark purple ridges on old trees.

Stone or umbrella pine

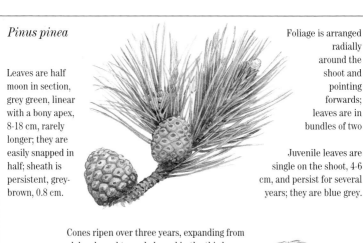

Pinus pinea

Leaves are half moon in section, grey green, linear with a bony apex, 8-18 cm, rarely longer; they are easily snapped in half; sheath is persistent, grey-brown, 0.8 cm.

Foliage is arranged radially around the shoot and pointing forwards; leaves are in bundles of two

Juvenile leaves are single on the shoot, 4-6 cm, and persist for several years; they are blue grey.

Cones ripen over three years, expanding from globe-shaped to oval-shaped in the third summer and ripening from green to shiny brown. They are knobbly. Scales are rounded with two scars on the dorsal knob.

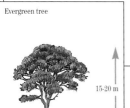

Seed is 2 cm, not winged, edible.

Evergreen tree

15-20 m

Stone pine is native to the Mediterranean region and the southern shore of the Black Sea. Its precise origin is confused, as it has been planted for thousands of years, but it is probably native to the eastern Mediterranean and only planted in the west. The seeds are an important food and were brought to Britain by the Romans, but only to eat: there is no record of it being planted before the 16th century. The alternative name of umbrella pine refers to the habit of mature trees. Height growth soon stops and the main branches form radiating spokes to support a dome of foliage, very similar to the design of an umbrella. The tree is unusual in retaining its juvenile foliage for several years. In most species, juvenile single leaves are only present for the first year. Another almost unique characteristic of stone pine is that the cones ripen over three years, as opposed to two years in all other pines, bar just one Mexican species. Fertilization occurs in the third spring. (Pine cones are pollinated in their first year, but the pollen does not fertilize the ovules until the second spring; after that the cones expand and mature.)

The short, stout bole, with a domed crown set on (umbrella shaped) radiating heavy branches, is highly characteristic of this tree.

BARK
Orange on young trees, soon fissuring to give deep furrows and long, scaly ridges of orange and pink brown.

Aleppo pine

Pinus halepensis

Foliage is sparse, arranged radially around the slender shoot and pointing forwards; leaves are in bundles of two.

Leaves are half moon in shape, fresh green, linear with a sharp tip, 6-11 cm; bundles are held in a persisting, dark grey sheath, 0.3-0.4 cm long.

Cone is 5-12 cm, oblong cone shaped and red brown when ripe in second year. It points back along the shoot or spreads, and is slow to open, unless exposed to a forest fire; scales are fairly smooth.

SIMILAR SPECIES
Pinus brutia

Calabrian pine's leaves are yellow green, sparse, 10-15 cm; bundles are held in a persistent, dark brown sheath, 0.7-1.5 cm long.

Calabrian pine's cone points forwards along the shoot or at a right angle to it. It is elongated, 5-11 cm, and bright brown.

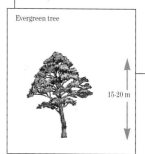

Evergreen tree

15-20 m

This pine is mainly native to the Mediterranean region from Greece west to the Iberian peninsula; it is also found in Morocco and Algeria. However, there is a small population around Aleppo in Syria, and in Israel. By a quirk of fate, the species was named after the Aleppo population, which is Latinized to give *Halepensis* ('-ensis' means 'comes from'). Aleppo pine is very tolerant of low rainfall and is used in forestry on dry sites in Spain and elsewhere in the Mediterranean region. The timber is a useful quality, and it produces resin.

Calabrian pine has a native distribution in north-eastern Greece, Crete, Cyprus, Turkey, Syria, Lebanon, the Crimea and the Ukraine. A variety is recorded from Azerbaijan east through Iran to Pakistan. There is a population in Calabria in southern Italy (the old Latin name for Calabria is Brutia). Whether it is native to Western Europe or an early introduction is unknown, but the species was named from the Calabrian trees. The tree is almost unique in having cones pointing forwards on the shoot. Only one other pine, Jack pine (*Pinus banksiana*, a relative of *P. contorta,* page 84), shares this feature.

This is essentially a small to medium sized tree. The foliage appears sparse rather than dense.

BARK
Smooth and silvery grey in young trees; later it is fissured, red brown and scaly on old trees.

Ponderosa pine

Pinus ponderosa

Leaves are triangular in section, grey-green, 11-22 cm long, stiff and linear. They have a bony point. Sheath persistent, brown, 1.2-1.6 cm. long.

Foliage is arranged radially around the stout grey-brown shoots; leaves are in bundles of three.

Cone is oval shaped in the first year, expanding in second summer when it may be oval cone shaped. It is purple brown, 6-16 cm long; scales are thin with a reflexed prickle. The cone falls after opening, leaving a ring of scales on the branch.

SIMILAR SPECIES
Pinus jeffreyi
Jeffrey pine's cones are cone to oval cone shaped, rounded at the base when closed, 13-25 cm by 5-8 cm (closed). Opening to 15 cm, they are red brown, falling once ripe, leaving a few scales on the branch.

Jeffrey pine's leaves grey green or bluish green, 12-26 cm long. Bundles are held in a persisting sheath 0.8 cm long. Leaves are set on stout, waxy bloomed grey green shoots.

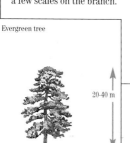

Evergreen tree

20-40 m

Ponderosa pine, also known as western yellow pine, is native to western North America from British Columbia to north-eastern California, although trees treated as related species or sub-species occur in the eastern flank of the Rocky Mountains and along the Pacific Coast ranges of Washington and California. It grows as a column, with short branches set off the stout trunk and carrying the bold foliage. This is a three-needled pine and, therefore, the leaves have two flat sides and one rounded side, allowing the leaves to come together to form a cylinder. The timber is a good quality and accounts for the alternative name of western yellow pine.

Jeffrey pine occurs from south-western Oregon through California and western Nevada to Baja California in northern Mexico. It is easily identified by the shoots, with their strong bloom with a waxy layer; and by its cones. Its resin is also different, containing the volatile element heptane, which could be purified to run a car. Jeffrey pine tends to occur on drier and poorer sites than ponderosa pine. In cultivation it has similarly bold foliage.

Ponderosa pine makes a majestic tree as here in a native stand in Washington east of Mount Rainier, where it grows with *Abies grandis* (page 74), *Pinus contorta* (page 84), *Pseudotsuga menziesii* (page 68), *Thuja plicata* (page 30), a *Larix* and a *Picea*.

BARK
Dark brown or purple grey on young trees, fissuring and developing broad flat scaly plates of orange brown and purple grey on old trees.

95

Monterey pine

Pinus radiata

Foliage is arranged radially around the grey-green to reddish-brown shoot; leaves are in bundles of three.

Leaves are triangular in section, grassy green, linear, soft and slender, 10-16 cm; bundles are held in a persistent pale brown sheath, 1-1.3 cm long.

Shoots are usually multi-nodal – with up to four nodes in a single spurt of growth.

Cones stay on the tree, only opening after forest fires or strong heat.

Cones are egg shaped and pale brown in the first year, expanding in the second year , 6-16 cm.There are usually around 20 large, rounded scales on the outer side of the cone; other side is much smoother.

Evergreen tree

25-35 m

Monterey pine, also known as radiata pine, is restricted in the wild to just five sites: three locations on the Californian coast (the most famous of which is the Monterey peninsula); and two islands off the coast of Baja California, Mexico. The trees on these two islands differ in having the leaves predominantly in pairs, not threes, and also in their cones, which are frequently without the score of large rounded scales on the outside. The woody projections on these scales are believed to be a protection against squirrels, as the tree builds up a reserve of seeds in the unopened cones, awaiting a forest fire. The cones may remain on the tree for up to 40 years, but the seeds only remain viable for around 20 years. Monterey pine has a reasonable timber, produced very quickly. Thus a tree, which in the wild occupies only a few thousand acres, has been planted over millions of acres in warm temperate parts of the world, especially in New Zealand but also in South Africa, Chile and Spain. In New Zealand a tree is recorded as growing to a height of 60 m in 37 years, although in Britain and Europe most trees stop at half this height.

Young trees grow fast and have spiky crowns before developing the picturesque rounded domes of old trees.

BARK
Purplish grey on young trees, darkening and becoming deeply furrowed with thick, broad ridges.

97

Blue pine

Pinus wallichiana

Leaves are triangular in section, 11-20 cm long, slender and soft, often kinked and bending down. They are dull blue to vivid blue (with a bloom), but occasionally grey green, waxy bands on the inner two flat surfaces only. Bundles are held in a reflexed sheath which falls over in the first winter.

RELATED SPECIES
Pinus strobus
Eastern white pine has 8-10cm, straight grey green leaves set on slender, shiny olive-brown shoots which are ridged and hairy behind the leaf bundles. Cones are ellipse shaped, 10-20 cm long

Foliage is arranged radially around the olive-green to grey-green shoot; leaves are in bundles of five.

Cones are on long, erect and cylindrical flower stalks, 3-6 cm in the first year, hanging down as they expand to an oval shape 10-30 cm. They are often curved in second year, when they are very resinous and bluish green until ripening brown. Scales have a blunt prickle at the tip.

Pinus peuce
Macedonian pine has grey-green leaves, 7-11 cm long, set on grey-brown hairless shoots. The mature cones are cylindrical, 10-16 cm, and curved.

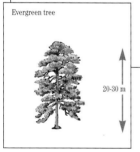

Evergreen tree

20-30 m

Blue pine occurs from eastern Afghanistan through Pakistan, southern Tibet, Nepal, Sikkim and Bhutan to north-eastern India, and is the dominant tree in the drier mountain valleys between 2,000 and 3,000 m. It is also known as Bhutan pine, although this name is best reserved for a related species which occurs from Bhutan to south-eastern Tibet. The best blue-foliaged trees occur at the western end of its range: in Bhutan itself, the trees tend to be grey-green in leaf, markedly less attractive. Like all soft pines, it has a quality timber without the marked differences between spring and summer wood found in the hard pines: easy to work. In soft pines, expansion of the first-year conelet occurs at the base of the scales, so the umbo or exposed portion of the first-year cone is terminal on the scale; in hard pines it is on the back (dorsal).

Eastern white pine or Weymouth pine (after a Captain Weymouth) is from eastern North America. It has one of the best timbers, but the foliage lacks the grace of blue pine. Macedonian pine is found in Albania, Bulgaria and Macedonia. It grows steadily, but not spectacularly, on a wide range of sites.

This shot (taken by the author in Bhutan) shows some of the characteristic blue-green foliage (see main text, opposite) but not as much as would a tree from the Western Himalayas.

BARK
Smooth and grey green on young trees, becoming fissured, dark grey or black and forming small scales.

Arolla pine

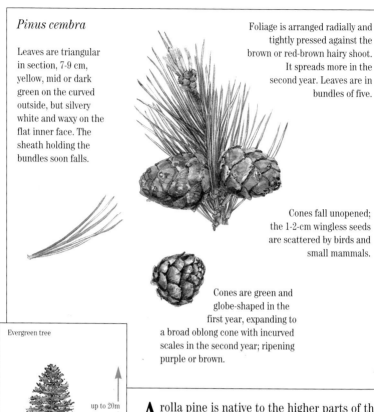

Pinus cembra

Leaves are triangular in section, 7-9 cm, yellow, mid or dark green on the curved outside, but silvery white and waxy on the flat inner face. The sheath holding the bundles soon falls.

Foliage is arranged radially and tightly pressed against the brown or red-brown hairy shoot. It spreads more in the second year. Leaves are in bundles of five.

Cones fall unopened; the 1-2-cm wingless seeds are scattered by birds and small mammals.

Cones are green and globe-shaped in the first year, expanding to a broad oblong cone with incurved scales in the second year; ripening purple or brown.

Evergreen tree

up to 20m

Arolla pine is native to the higher parts of the Alps and Carpathian ranges of Central Europe, where, in subalpine forests, it either forms pure stands or is mixed with European larch, *Larix decidua* (page 50). It is also known as Swiss stone pine, which is a reference to the large edible seeds. Actually, all pine seeds are edible, but only a few, such as those of arolla pine and umbrella pine, are sufficiently large to be worth while.

Arolla pine belongs to a small group of the soft pines in which the scales do not open to release the seeds. Instead, the whole cone falls intact to the ground where birds and small animals break them open in order to eat or carry off the seeds. Most are eaten sooner or later, but enough are missed to perpetuate the species. Arolla pine is not an important timber tree due to its subalpine habitat, although the timber is good. It is too slow growing in cultivation to be suitable for forestry plantations. As with most soft pines, the breathing pores or stomata are only found on the flat inner surfaces of the needles and not on the curved outside surface.

Most pines lose their lower branches as they mature, but given enough light on an open situation (as here) arolla pine can keep live branches to ground level.

BARK
Dark grey and smooth on young trees, developing fissures which expose red-brown and scaly ridges.

A key to broadleaved trees

'Broadleaved' is a useful enough term. This group of trees generally does have much narrower leaves than conifers. They are also known as hardwoods, as opposed to the conifers, which are known as softwoods. Such generalizations don't cover every single case, but most broadleaved trees do have harder or denser timber than the conifers.

The broadleaved trees belong to a larger number of botanical families than the conifers. The 45 genera illustrated as main species in this section of the guide belong to 25 families, compared to six families and 21 genera in the conifers.

The order of species in this section is **firstly** by **leaf shape**, with a progression from simple shapes to more complex ones, and only **secondly** by **botanical character**.

Sessile oak.

Simplest leaf shapes
Pages 106-217 and 238-239

The leaves of these species are either without lobes, or the lobes are extensions of side veins which branch off the central vein.

However, related species are placed together. So, all the oaks follow each other (pages 148-161), even though there are obvious visual differences between, for example, sessile oak, holm oak and red oak.

Wild service tree (pages 238-239) is next to rowan (pages 240-241) and service tree (pages 242-243) because of their botanical relationships.

White poplar (pages 134-135) has been put in this group, even though its veins place it in the next group, because of its close similarity to aspen (pages 132-133) and their mutual hybrid, grey poplar.

Simplest leaf shapes: Turkish hazel.

Palmate leaves
Pages 222-239

In these trees the main leaf veins arise at, or are close to, the top end of the leaf stalk; they also run to the tips of the lobes. This distinctive leaf shape is called palmate, because the veins start together from the base in the same way that our fingers actually start at the wrist. Normally there are three, five or seven lobes on these leaves, although in *Catalpa* (pages 218-219) and Paulownia (pages 220-221) only some leaves have lobes.

Compound leaves
Pages 240-279

Most have pinnately compound leaves: that is, the leaf is divided into a number (almost always an odd number) of leaflets

Compound leaves: walnut.

or little leaves, which arise successively along the stalk. Pages 266-271 cover bi-pinnate (or doubly pinnate) leaves in which the leaflets themselves may be divided into leaflets. Honey locust (pages 266-267) may have either pinnate or bi-pinnate leaves on the same branch. Horse chestnut (pages 272-273) is palmately compound, with the leaflets originating as a cluster from one point.

Very large leaves
Pages 274-279

These cover the palms, with their enormous leaves.

Back section – shrubs, or shrub-like trees
Pages 281-283

This short final section comprises a selection of shrubs or shrub-like trees, frequently growing on more than one stem.

Palmate leaves: London plane.

A key to broadleaved trees/2

Fruits and seeds
Besides covering leaf shape, this guide
also describes fruits and seeds that are
likely to help identify a tree.

Pear.

Is it fleshy?
This is the simplest test. Can you stick
your thumbnail into the fruit? Pages 174-
191, 196-201, 204-205, 210-213, 216-217,
238-243, 250-251, 254-255 and 274-279 all
have fleshy fruits. Of these, keaki (pages
174-175), the magnolias (pages 210-213)
and varnish tree (pages 254-255) have
rather thin fleshy layers, which quickly
become dry; in walnut (pages 250-251)
the fleshy layer soon opens to show the
hard nut, which may well break your
thumbnail. Fruits such as cherry are on
pages 180-185 and 196-199; apple and
pear are on pages 184-191 and 238-243.

Cork oak.

**Does the fruit sit in a cup, or is it
enclosed by one?**
See the beech family (which includes
oaks) on pages 148-165 and also Turkish
hazel (pages 122-123).

**Is the fruit
cluster obviously
winged?**
The elms (pages
166-173), ashes
(pages 244-249)
and the tree of
heaven (pages 256-257) have seeds
either in the middle of a round wing (the
elms) or have a wing which tapers
around the seed.

Wych elm.

The maples (pages 226-237 and pages
258-259) have a fruit with the seed
sitting very clearly at one end of the
wing (and in pairs on the fruit clusters).
Wingnut (pages 252-253) has two small
wings. In hornbeam and hop hornbeam
(pages 124-127), the seed sits in a wing-
like scale.

**Is the fruit like
a flattened pea
pod?**
This is
characteristic of
the legume
family (pages
202-203 and 260-
269).

Flattened pod.

**Is the fruit a
catkin?**
Alder or birch
(pages 106-121)
have catkins; so
do poplars and
willows (pages
128-147 and 280-
281). But also
check hornbeam
and hop
hornbeam (pages
124-127), as
these also have
catkins.

Alder catkin.

Is the fruit a capsule which opens along the side to release seeds?
Catalpa and *Paulownia* (pages 218-221) release winged seeds. Eucalypts (pages 206-209) release small seeds from holes at the top of the fruit. Horse chestnut (pages 272-273) and pride of India (pages 274-275) also have capsules.

Capsule.

Tulip tree.

If the tree is none of these, check tulip tree (pages 214-215), limes (pages 192-195), plane (pages 222-223) and *Liquidambar* pages (224-225).

Identifying trees in winter

There are several easy ways to narrow down the possibilities when the leaves have fallen:

Shoots and buds are the most useful characters, often narrowing the choices down to at least which genus.

Look first at the arrangement of the buds. Most trees have

Buds set alternately.

Buds in opposite pairs.

the buds set alternately along the shoot, but in phillyrea (pages 196-197), olive (pages 198-199), eucalypts (pages 206-209), *Catalpa* (pages 218-219), *Paulownia* (pages 220-221), maples (pages 226-235 and 258-9), ash (pages 244-249) and horse chestnut (pages 272-273), they are in opposite pairs or threes.

Winter silhouette, wild service tree.

This character should always be the first to check because trees with similar leaves, such as maples and *Liquidambar,* ash and rowan, have different bud arrangements.

In winter you will often find leaves from last summer caught up somewhere around the tree. Similarly, look at any fruits remaining on the tree or scattered around it, or debris, perhaps the cup of an acorn.

Crack willow: single bud scale.

Also look for any special or unusual character, whether in the bark (such as peeling bark of birches, pages 114-121); root suckers (the only maple species which suckers is Cappadocian maple, pages 230-231); or buds –

Grey alder: stalked buds.

willows (pages 134-147), have only a single bud scale. Alders (pages 106-113) – except green alder – have stalked buds with two scales. Wingnut (pages 252-253) has naked buds where next year's leaves are exposed in miniature, or twigs (shoots). Only walnut (pages 250-251) and wingnut (pages 252-253) have a chambered pith. These are just a few of the commonest examples.

Alder

Alnus glutinosa

Leaf is shiny deep green on top, initially with sticky glands; underside is pale green with tufts of white hairs in the axils of the veins, of which there are six to eight pairs. Leaves are 4-10 cm by 3-7 cm; leaf stalk is 1.5-3.5 cm.

Leaves grow alternately on the shoot, and are broadly egg shaped (narrow end attached) to nearly rounded; the base is wedge shaped, the tip is rounded and often notched, the margin is wavy with irregular teeth.

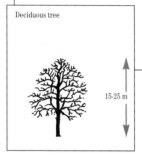

Shoot is initially covered by sticky glands, maturing to grey; buds are oblong, with two scales covered with small grey scales, 0.7 cm, set on a scaly stalk, 0.5 cm long.

Catkins, 2-3 cm long, are exposed over winter. They open in late winter. At first purple, they shed yellow pollen and expand to 7 cm. Female flowers are egg shaped, red purple, in clusters of four to five. Fruit is an egg- or globe-shaped woody catkin, ripening from green to blackish brown; 1.2-1.5 cm long.

Deciduous tree

15-25 m

Alder is native throughout Europe except for the far north and Iceland, the Faroe Isles, Crete and the Balearic Islands. It is also found in North Africa. In the east, it extends into the Caucasus. Over this range it shows some variation, with plants on Corsica having small, nearly circular leaves set on red-brown twigs, while those from the Caucasus have leaves rounded at the base with eight to ten pairs of veins and hairy shoots.

Alder grows mainly along streams and rivers, or in wet flushes where a spring emerges. It can form forests or copses on waterlogged sites, known as alder carrs. It will grow if planted on drier sites, but normally cannot establish as a seedling. The Latin name refers to the clammy glands on the new leaves and shoots, which later dry to black warts. The timber is light and easily worked, hence its historic use for clogs. When fresh it is white, but on exposure to the air it dries to reddish brown. It has little natural durability, except when kept under water. It produces good charcoal, considered the best for gunpowder. Alders will readily coppice if cut down. Old alders on river banks have often been coppiced.

Coppiced alders in their typical habitat (see main text, opposite). The purple cast is caused by the unexpanded male catkins (see artwork panel, opposite). The photograph was taken in February.

BARK
Purplish brown on young trees, maturing to grey brown and developing orange or pale fissures. On old trees it cracks into small, grey vertical plates.

Grey alder

Alnus incana

Leaf is dull green on top, underside is grey and hairy, especially on the nine to 12 pairs of veins, leaf is 5-10 cm by 4-6 cm; leaf stalk is 2.5-3 cm.

Leaves grow alternately on the shoot, and are oval to egg shaped. Base is wedge shaped to rounded; untoothed except at the base. Apex is pointed. Margin has usually six triangular lobes or coarse teeth with small teeth between.

Catkins, 2-3 cm long, are exposed over winter, opening in late winter. They are purple red with yellow pollen and expand to 10 cm. Female flowers are red-purple in clusters of three to eight.

Shoot is grey or grey brown, initially with a grey down. Buds are oblong, with two bud scales. Seed is small and narrowly winged.

Fruit is an egg-shaped woody catkin, ripening to a dark colour in the first autumn, 1.2-2.2 cm long.

Deciduous tree

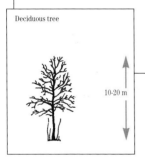

10-20 m

Grey alder is native to Central and northern Europe, and the Caucasus. It is found along streams and rivers, but requires better drainage than common alder and does not grow in water or waterlogged sites. It prefers chalk or limestone sites and will grow, when planted, on drier sites than most other alders. It is unusual in that it sends out suckers from the roots, so mature trees are usually surrounded by a ring of saplings. The tree is useful in orchards, where it is planted to protect blossom from late spring frosts: it comes into leaf early providing shelter, while the narrow crown and light foliage do not compete with the fruit trees for water and nutrients.

Alders have a symbiotic relationship with a group of bacteria which allows them to fix atmospheric nitrogen into a form which they can use to make proteins. This ability to acquire nitrogen from the air, not just from the soil, allows alders to grow on poor soils: so they are used on land reclamation sites to add nitrogen and leaf litter, and thus to improve the soil.

This tree is typically narrow crowned, with sparse rather than dense branching. It is dull green, as opposed to the brilliant green of Italian alder, page 110).

BARK
Dark grey and smooth in young trees, with vertical breathing pores (lenticels). On older trees it is dull grey and fissured.

Italian alder

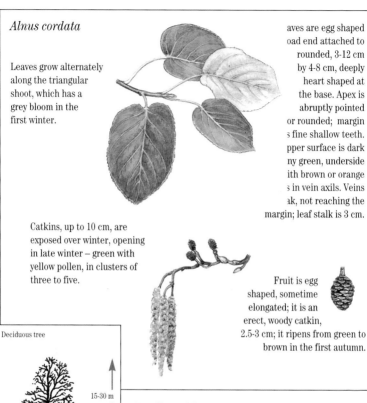

Alnus cordata

Leaves grow alternately along the triangular shoot, which has a grey bloom in the first winter.

...aves are egg shaped ...oad end attached to rounded, 3-12 cm by 4-8 cm, deeply heart shaped at the base. Apex is abruptly pointed or rounded; margin ...s fine shallow teeth. ...pper surface is dark ...ny green, underside ...ith brown or orange ...s in vein axils. Veins ...ak, not reaching the margin; leaf stalk is 3 cm.

Catkins, up to 10 cm, are exposed over winter, opening in late winter – green with yellow pollen, in clusters of three to five.

Fruit is egg shaped, sometime elongated; it is an erect, woody catkin, 2.5-3 cm; it ripens from green to brown in the first autumn.

Deciduous tree

15-30 m

Italian alder is native to southern Italy and Corsica, also north-western Albania. The Italian form is the one commonly cultivated.

Corsican specimens have rounded tips to the leaves, as opposed to pointed. Leaves of Albanian trees are at the bottom end of the size range given above. The southern origin of Italian alder belies its hardiness, with trees nearly 30 m in height being found as far north as southern Scotland. Like many of Europe's native trees, it probably has not recolonized land lost during the most recent Ice Age. In cultivation, it quickly makes a tree 10 m high, but grows more slowly after that. It is attractive for its dense glossy foliage and colourful catkins which open on the bare boughs in late winter or early spring. It is relatively narrow, which makes it suitable for streets. Its only drawback is the lack of any autumn colour. It will grow on a wide range of soils, tolerating dry ones better than most alders. The timber is light, but suitable for packing and plywood. It is also very durable, especially under water, because of the preservative chemicals in it. The piles on which Venice rests are of alder – possibly this very species.

The typical dense crown of Italian alder gives it a superficial similarity to a pear tree – but it is readily separated by the small, woody cones – see the artwork panel, opposite.

BARK
Is smooth, with blisters, grey brown to grey on young trees; later it is fissured at the base.

Green alder

Alnus viridis

Leaves are egg shaped to rounded oval, 2.5-8 cm by 2-7 cm; the apex is acute, base rounded, margin doubly toothed. Triangular teeth and hairs can be found in the intervening sinuses. Upper surface is green (a dull sheen) with impressed hairy veins; underside is pale shiny green and sticky, with black glandular dots on the six to eight pairs of veins. There are brown hairs in the axils. Leaf stalk is 1.5 cm.

Catkins have white resin over winter, and expand with the new leaves in April/May to 5-8 cm.

Leaves grow alternately along the brown shoot, which is strongly ridged below the leaves.

Fruit is an egg-shaped woody catkin, ripening from green to dark brown in the first autumn, 1.2-2 cm.

Buds are lance shaped, with many pressed-down scales. They are shiny green or purple, and have no stalk.

Deciduous shrubby tree

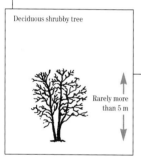

Rarely more than 5 m

Green alder is native to the mountains of Central and south-eastern Europe. It is unlike the other alders featured in this guide in several ways, being the type of a separate sub-genus *Alnobetula*. Its buds are pointed, with many pressed-down (imbricate) scales; and the buds have no stalk (though those at the base of the shoot may have a slight stalk). The fact that green alder is more of a shrub than a tree is a practical difference, rather than a botanical one. It shares, with its larger cousins, many of the typical alder characteristics, for example, nitrogen-fixing bacteria (see page 108); male and female catkins exposed over winter before expanding in the spring; and a fruit which is a woody catkin (often termed a cone). This is very similar to birch tree's fruit; however, alder fruit is persistent, while birch fruit disintegrates to release the seeds.

Green alder is used as a nurse species in forest plantations and land reclamation sites to provide shelter and nitrogen, while not growing so large as to compete with crop trees.

Green alder makes a tanglewood rather than a forest in mountain thickets.

BARK
Brown and smooth.

Silver birch

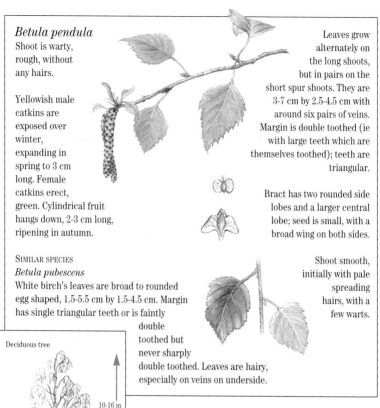

Betula pendula
Shoot is warty, rough, without any hairs.

Yellowish male catkins are exposed over winter, expanding in spring to 3 cm long. Female catkins erect, green. Cylindrical fruit hangs down, 2-3 cm long, ripening in autumn.

SIMILAR SPECIES
Betula pubescens
White birch's leaves are broad to rounded egg shaped, 1.5-5.5 cm by 1.5-4.5 cm. Margin has single triangular teeth or is faintly double toothed but never sharply double toothed. Leaves are hairy, especially on veins on underside.

Leaves grow alternately on the long shoots, but in pairs on the short spur shoots. They are 3-7 cm by 2.5-4.5 cm with around six pairs of veins. Margin is double toothed (ie with large teeth which are themselves toothed); teeth are triangular.

Bract has two rounded side lobes and a larger central lobe; seed is small, with a broad wing on both sides.

Shoot smooth, initially with pale spreading hairs, with a few warts.

Deciduous tree

10-16 m

Silver birch is native throughout Europe from the Pyrenees and Britain east into northern Asia. It grows on light well drained soils, making a fast growing small tree which rarely lives for more than 50 years. The wood is light and used to make birch plywood. In spring the sap contains sugars and can be tapped to make beer or wine. The silvery whiteness in the trunk is caused by betulin.

White birch has a similar range to silver birch (but is the only tree native to Iceland) and is superficially very similar. The leaves are singly toothed, that is with teeth of a similar size, while silver birch has large triangular teeth with several smaller teeth. The leaves are also hairy and the shoots are hairy with or without warts. However, the bark never develops the corky ridges so characteristic of silver birch. The names white and brown birch refer to the bark colour, whilst downy birch refers to the hairy shoots and leaves. While white birch is a boardly similar tree to silver birch, they rarely interbreed because of genetic differences. It grows on wetter sites than silver birch, although they often occur together.

Silver birch makes a graceful tree with a light delicate crown, usually turning a beautiful yellow in autumn.

BARK
Silvery white in the upper crown. On old trees it fissures to give thick, corky ridges at the base.

Paper birch or canoe birch

Betula papyrifera

Leaves grow alternately or in small whorls on spur shoots. They are a triangular egg shape, 5-10 cm by 3-5 cm, tapering to a point and rounded or shallow heart shaped at the base. Margin has acute double teeth. Underside has black glands and shows the five to ten pairs of veins and hairs in vein axils. Leaf stalk, 1.5-2.5 cm, has little black dots (glands).

Shoot is either hairy or hairless, with or without warts.

Male catkins are yellow in spring, when they expand to 6-10 cm. Cylindrical, hanging fruit is 4-5 cm long.

Deciduous tree

Up to 10-20 m

Paper birch has an extensive native range across North America from the Atlantic coast of Canada almost to the Pacific Ocean in Alaska, and in the east down the Appalachian Mountains to New York and Pennsylvania. Trees vary across this range, especially in the bark colour. Occasional forms exist which are slow to lose the juvenile brown bark. The trunks can grow large enough for the timber mill, but in Europe the species is primarily used as an ornamental tree.

As suggested by the name, the most important feature of this tree was the bark. It can be peeled in thin sheets (taking care not to remove the bottom layer, which can damage the tree). Because they contain betulin (the white, waxy constituent of birch bark), the sheets are waterproof, and were used by native Americans to cover their canoes. The sheets were also used as paper, which is the translation of the Latin name.

Paper birch is generally similar to silver and white birch, and is planted in parks and gardens. The best identifier is the quantity of black dots (resin glands) on the underside of the leaves.

Paper birch is used as an ornamental tree for its attractive bark and golden autumn colour.

BARK
Becomes creamy white to chalky white, but often with a pinkish hint; it is brown on young trees.

River birch

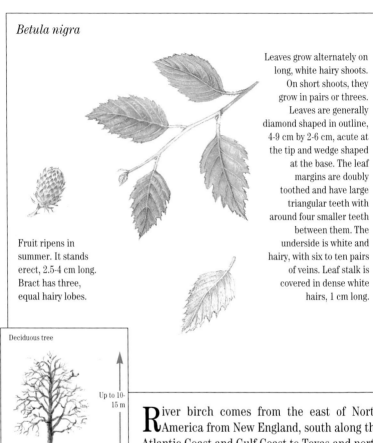

Betula nigra

Leaves grow alternately on long, white hairy shoots. On short shoots, they grow in pairs or threes. Leaves are generally diamond shaped in outline, 4-9 cm by 2-6 cm, acute at the tip and wedge shaped at the base. The leaf margins are doubly toothed and have large triangular teeth with around four smaller teeth between them. The underside is white and hairy, with six to ten pairs of veins. Leaf stalk is covered in dense white hairs, 1 cm long.

Fruit ripens in summer. It stands erect, 2.5-4 cm long. Bract has three, equal hairy lobes.

Deciduous tree

Up to 10-15 m

River birch comes from the east of North America from New England, south along the Atlantic Coast and Gulf Coast to Texas and north to Wisconsin: the most southerly of the American birch species. It is a tree of wet places, restricted through most of its range to boggy riverside sites which flood at periods of high water. In cultivation it will happily grow on most soils. However, the ripening of the fruit in summer is related to its natural habitat: the water level is lowest during the summer and, therefore, the seeds are produced at this time, so they can germinate in the damp soil before being inundated.

River birch is also known as black birch, a reference to the bark of very old trees which becomes black and flakes in small scales. However, most trees in cultivation in Britain and Europe are much younger and only show the buff or orange-whitish bark, which has a betulin content and flakes attractively.

The erect fruits, the white, hairy diamond-shaped leaves and the shoots, which are covered in dense white hairs when young, help to distinguish river birch from other birches.

River birch makes an attractive ornamental tree. Old trees have an unusual bark – see right In the U.K. there are only a very few old trees.

BARK
Buff pink or orange on young trees, developing large peeling flakes. On old trees, it becomes black or reddish and develops peeling flakes.

Himalayan birch

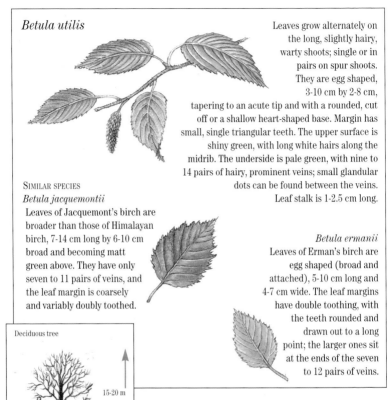

Betula utilis

Leaves grow alternately on the long, slightly hairy, warty shoots; single or in pairs on spur shoots. They are egg shaped, 3-10 cm by 2-8 cm, tapering to an acute tip and with a rounded, cut off or a shallow heart-shaped base. Margin has small, single triangular teeth. The upper surface is shiny green, with long white hairs along the midrib. The underside is pale green, with nine to 14 pairs of hairy, prominent veins; small glandular dots can be found between the veins. Leaf stalk is 1-2.5 cm long.

SIMILAR SPECIES

Betula jacquemontii
Leaves of Jacquemont's birch are broader than those of Himalayan birch, 7-14 cm long by 6-10 cm broad and becoming matt green above. They have only seven to 11 pairs of veins, and the leaf margin is coarsely and variably doubly toothed.

Betula ermanii
Leaves of Erman's birch are egg shaped (broad and attached), 5-10 cm long and 4-7 cm wide. The leaf margins have double toothing, with the teeth rounded and drawn out to a long point; the larger ones sit at the ends of the seven to 12 pairs of veins.

Deciduous tree

15-20 m

This tree is native to the Himalayas from central Nepal east through India, Bhutan and Burma to western China. It forms forests up to the tree-line, but also grows in mixed forests with magnolia, *Tsuga*, *Abies* and rhododendron where the birches with the best barks are found. In old, undisturbed trees, the thin layers of bark can hang on the trees as sheets up to 0.6 m across. The Latin name translates as 'useful': it provides timber and firewood, while the sheets of bark are used by local people as paper.

Jacquemont's birch occurs along the Himalayas west from central Nepal through India and Pakistan to eastern Afghanistan. It is often treated as a variety of Himalayan birch, to which it is similar but easily separated by the white bark and the broader egg-shaped leaves which have double teeth and fewer veins. It shares characteristics with the silver birch group of species.

Erman's birch is native to Japan, Korea, north-eastern China and Russia from Lake Baikal to Kamchatka. It shares the white bark of Jacquemont's birch, but this peels away in small strips, not large sheets.

Himalayan birch makes a domed crown. In the Himalayas (this photograph was taken in Bhutan) it may grow in mixed forest with other trees (see main text, opposite) and bamboo, as here.

BARK

Himalayan birch's bark is red brown to copper brown and without any waxy bloom. It peels in thin sheets. Bark of Jacquemont's birch and Erman's birch is white or creamy white and extending up into the branches.

Turkish hazel

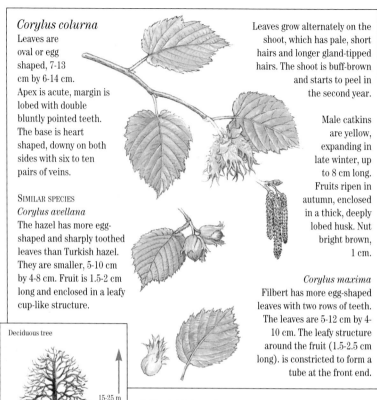

Corylus colurna
Leaves are oval or egg shaped, 7-13 cm by 6-14 cm. Apex is acute, margin is lobed with double bluntly pointed teeth. The base is heart shaped, downy on both sides with six to ten pairs of veins.

SIMILAR SPECIES
Corylus avellana
The hazel has more egg-shaped and sharply toothed leaves than Turkish hazel. They are smaller, 5-10 cm by 4-8 cm. Fruit is 1.5-2 cm long and enclosed in a leafy cup-like structure.

Deciduous tree

15-25 m

Leaves grow alternately on the shoot, which has pale, short hairs and longer gland-tipped hairs. The shoot is buff-brown and starts to peel in the second year.

Male catkins are yellow, expanding in late winter, up to 8 cm long. Fruits ripen in autumn, enclosed in a thick, deeply lobed husk. Nut bright brown, 1 cm.

Corylus maxima
Filbert has more egg-shaped leaves with two rows of teeth. The leaves are 5-12 cm by 4-10 cm. The leafy structure around the fruit (1.5-2.5 cm long). is constricted to form a tube at the front end.

Turkish hazel grows in the wild from southeastern Europe across to western Turkey and into the Caucasus and northern Iran. It forms a narrow conical or column-shaped crown with regular spreading branches. Its tolerance of poor soils, makes it a useful street tree. The nuts are too small to be sold.

Hazel is found throughout most of Europe and extends east into the Caucasus and Turkey. Although it can make a trunk 25 cm in diameter and grows up to 8 m, it is more commonly found as a shrub with six to ten or more slender stems. It was often grown as a coppice, that is, cut down to ground level so it sprouts from the base. This may be repeated each ten to 15 years for centuries. The stems are harvested when 5-8 cm in diameter, split and woven into wattles, or used for poles or firewood. Wattles were used as enclosures for sheep, and as the framework on to which mud or plaster was daubed to make walls – hence wattle and daub. The nuts are tasty and known as cob nuts.

Filbert is native to south-eastern Europe and Turkey, and makes a small shrubby tree. It is cultivated for its large nuts.

Turkish hazel's typical leafy, cone-shaped crown in summer. The tree brightens in late winter when the male catkins open and hang down from the branches.

BARK
The unusual and attractive bark is buff brown or ash grey, becoming thick, fissured and scaly on old trees.

Hornbeam

Carpinus betulus

Leaves are egg shaped (broad end attached) to oval, 5-9 cm by 2.5-5 cm. They taper to a pointed tip and are rounded or heart shaped at the base. Margin has triangular, coarse double toothing. Upper surface is matt green and slightly hairy on the indented veins; underside is pale shiny green with ten to 15 pairs of veins.

<small>SIMILAR SPECIES</small>
Carpinus orientalis
Oriental hornbeam's leaves are smaller, 2-6 cm long by 1.2-2.5 cm. They have regular double teeth, and are pointed, with ten to 14 pairs of silky, downy veins.

Leaves grow alternately on the shoots. The shoots are slender and initially hairy, ripening from green to brown. Buds are egg shaped and pointed, 0.4-0.7 cm.

Fruits develop in pairs along a hanging catkin. Each fruit comprises a leafy bract 2.5-4 cm long, with a large oblong middle lobe and two spreading side lobes. It contains a ribbed seed 0.7 cm long.

The fruit of oriental hornbeam has triangular oval to egg-shaped bracts, 1.5-2 cm long. They are coarsely toothed on both sides, but not lobed.

Deciduous tree

15-25 m

This is native to the area from south-eastern England across Europe to Turkey. The common name is derived from two old English words, 'horn' meaning hard, and 'beam', meaning tree. The very tough timber is not easily worked, but serves as chopping boards and the like. Once, it was used for making yokes for oxen. The scientific name refers to its relationship with the birches. Unlike birch, however, the male catkins are enclosed in the buds over winter and this characteristic also separates it from the more closely related *Ostrya* genus.

Hornbeam is superficially very similar to beech, especially in the silvery grey and smooth bark. However, it makes a smaller tree, has much smaller buds and the fruit is very different. It also tolerates heavier and less well-drained soils. Like beech, it retains its dead leaves over the winter period when young, so it can be used to make a dense hedge. The cultivar *fastigiata* is commonly planted in streets and parks.

Oriental hornbeam occurs from Italy east to the Caucasus. It is a much smaller tree and tolerates drier sites.

Hornbeam is a tree of heavy clay soils, where it occurs either in mixed forests or hedgerows. This photograph shows the cultivar *fastigiata* (see main text, opposite).

BARK
Smooth and silvery grey throughout the tree's life, although fluted on older trees.

Hop hornbeam

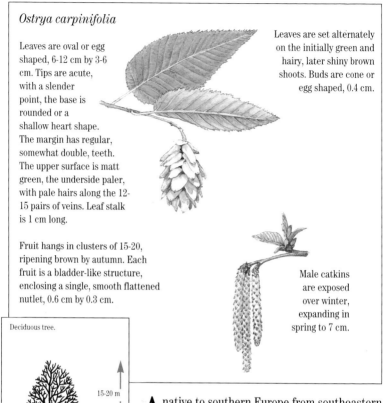

Ostrya carpinifolia

Leaves are oval or egg shaped, 6-12 cm by 3-6 cm. Tips are acute, with a slender point, the base is rounded or a shallow heart shape. The margin has regular, somewhat double, teeth. The upper surface is matt green, the underside paler, with pale hairs along the 12-15 pairs of veins. Leaf stalk is 1 cm long.

Fruit hangs in clusters of 15-20, ripening brown by autumn. Each fruit is a bladder-like structure, enclosing a single, smooth flattened nutlet, 0.6 cm by 0.3 cm.

Leaves are set alternately on the initially green and hairy, later shiny brown shoots. Buds are cone or egg shaped, 0.4 cm.

Male catkins are exposed over winter, expanding in spring to 7 cm.

Deciduous tree.

15-20 m

A native to southern Europe from southeastern France across to Asia Minor and north into the Caucasus, hop hornbean occurs on dry hillsides in mixed broadleafed forest. The 'hop' in the common name refers to the similarity of the fruit to that of the hop used to flavour beer and lager, but unfortunately cannot be used to such good effect.

The seeds are completely enclosed in their bladder-like shell, and the generic name *Ostrya* is from the Greek for a shell. The tree is closely related to the hornbeams, sharing similar foliage and a timber of similar hardness, put to similar uses. *Ostrya* can be separated from the hornbeams when in fruit by the bladder and, when not in fruit, by the male catkins, exposed from when they are formed in the summer until they expand in the spring. On hornbeams, they are enclosed within the buds.

Hop hornbeam makes an attractive tree, both in the wild and in cultivation, flourishing on all well-drained soils. It is particularly effective when the male catkins expand in the spring and when the foliage turns yellow in autumn.

Hop hornbeam looks dense and leafy in early summer, as this photograph shows. It has good autumn colour and is attractive in early spring when the catkins expand.

BARK
Smooth and grey-green on young trees, becoming fissured and developing coarse scaly plates which reveal an orange brown beneath.

Aspen

Populus tremula

Leaves are round to egg shaped (broad end attached) in outline, 1.5-8 cm long and wide. Tip is rounded, base is rounded or a shallow heart shape. Margin is scalloped between the large rounded teeth. Upper surface is bluish green, underside bloomed or pale green. Young leaves have white hairs and are usually copper coloured. Leaf stalk is 4-8 cm, rounded near the base, but flattened near the blade, allowing it to move in the slightest breeze.

Leaves are set alternately along the shoots, which are shiny olive green, later brown. Buds are oval to cone-shaped, shiny brown, 0.6 cm.

Male flowers are on shoots which are ridged behind the egg-shaped buds. They open in spring and are 5-10 cm long.

SIMILAR SPECIES
Populus tremuloides
Leaves of American aspen have much finer teeth than aspen (*P. tremula*).

Deciduous tree

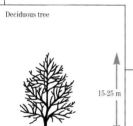

15-25 m

Aspen is native throughout Europe from northern Spain and Britain into Turkey and Central Asia; it is also in northern Algeria. It is restricted to moist sites, but once established can reproduce by suckers from the root system, and a single plant spreads over a large area. Aspen also reproduces by seed, which is light and blown by the wind. As with most poplars, there are male and female trees.

The shape of the leaf stalk or petiole allows the leaves to move in the slightest breeze, causing both movement and noise as the stiff leaves rattle together, and explains the common name of 'quaking aspen'. (The scientific name also alludes to this characteristic.) The timber is soft, burning slowly without spitting, and is used to make matches.

American aspen is found throughout North America south into northern Mexico. It is easily separated by the much finer toothing of the leaves. In north-eastern North America there is a related species, *Populus grandidentata*, which has much more coarsely toothed leaves. Both these American species are planted occasionally in Europe or used to produce hybrid poplars.

Aspen makes a tree with a column-shaped crown and is often surrounded by root suckers. Its autumn colour can be stunning – as seen here.

BARK
Smooth and greyish green on young trees, with prominent breathing pores (lenticels). It develops shallow ridges at the base of old trees.

European black poplar

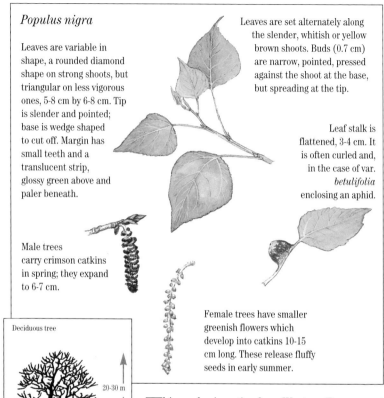

Populus nigra

Leaves are variable in shape, a rounded diamond shape on strong shoots, but triangular on less vigorous ones, 5-8 cm by 6-8 cm. Tip is slender and pointed; base is wedge shaped to cut off. Margin has small teeth and a translucent strip, glossy green above and paler beneath.

Leaves are set alternately along the slender, whitish or yellow brown shoots. Buds (0.7 cm) are narrow, pointed, pressed against the shoot at the base, but spreading at the tip.

Leaf stalk is flattened, 3-4 cm. It is often curled and, in the case of var. *betulifolia* enclosing an aphid.

Male trees carry crimson catkins in spring; they expand to 6-7 cm.

Deciduous tree

20-30 m

Female trees have smaller greenish flowers which develop into catkins 10-15 cm long. These release fluffy seeds in early summer.

This poplar is native from Western Europe east into Central Asia and south into North Africa. Over this area it has been much planted, and where it is truly native is open to question. This problem is illustrated by two of the commonly cultivated forms: First, Lombardy poplar, with its distinctive obelisk shape, bears two names which relate it to the Lombard region of northern Italy – the cultivar name is 'Italica'. However, it is not believed to be native to Italy but introduced from Central Asia. In its true form it is a male tree (the somewhat broader-crowned trees are female). Second, the Manchester poplar, which is var. *betulifolia*, from Western Europe, has a rounded, domed crown like a typical black poplar, but more dense and twiggy, and the leaves and leaf stalks are initially hairy. It is probably native to lowland England, but is mainly found as a male tree. Galls made by *Pemphigus* aphids are characteristic of this tree.

Black poplar was once widely cultivated for its timber, used for wagon bottoms as its softness absorbed shocks. Since the 1700s it has been supplanted by its hybrid with the North American eastern cottonwood.

130

Lombardy poplar is the most commonly seen form of black poplar, often planted well away from the damp riverside habits normally favoured by the species.

BARK
Grey-brown, developing deep fissures with short broad ridges; often with burrs.

Black cottonwood

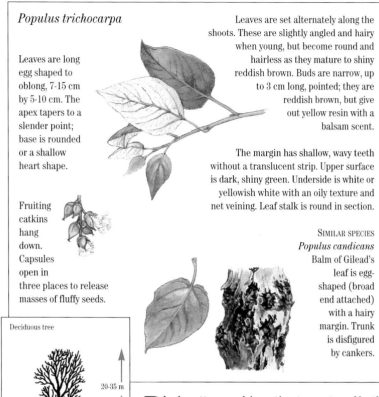

Populus trichocarpa

Leaves are long egg shaped to oblong, 7-15 cm by 5-10 cm. The apex tapers to a slender point; base is rounded or a shallow heart shape.

Fruiting catkins hang down. Capsules open in three places to release masses of fluffy seeds.

Deciduous tree

20-35 m

Leaves are set alternately along the shoots. These are slightly angled and hairy when young, but become round and hairless as they mature to shiny reddish brown. Buds are narrow, up to 3 cm long, pointed; they are reddish brown, but give out yellow resin with a balsam scent.

The margin has shallow, wavy teeth without a translucent strip. Upper surface is dark, shiny green. Underside is white or yellowish white with an oily texture and net veining. Leaf stalk is round in section.

SIMILAR SPECIES
Populus candicans
Balm of Gilead's leaf is egg-shaped (broad end attached) with a hairy margin. Trunk is disfigured by cankers.

Black cottonwood is native to western North America from Alaska south to Baja California of northern Mexico and inland to Alberta, Montana and South Dakota. It forms a neat column-shaped, crowned tree with a dense, leafy habit and turns yellow in autumn. It is grown as a specimen, and, like other poplars, likes damp sites. It has the light, soft timber typical of poplars.

The common name cottonwood refers to the cotton (strands of cellulose) which are attached to the small seeds and helps them to disperse in the wind. Only female poplars produce seeds, and are much unloved by those who hang out their washing in June: the seeds stick to damp clothes. Another common name for the tree is western balsam poplar: its new foliage has a strong balsam scent. The second word in the Latin name translates as 'hairy fruit'.

Balm of Gilead is a female tree of uncertain origin. It may be a form of the eastern balsam poplar (from eastern North America), or a hybrid of this with *Populus deltoides*. It makes a smaller-growing tree with beautiful balsam-scented foliage. It is often grown as the clone 'Aurora'.

Black cottonwood forms a column-shaped crown and often suckers at the base.

BARK
Grey green or yellowish grey and smooth, but on older trees turns greyer and fissures.

White poplar

Populus alba

Shoots are a vivid white and woolly when young; but the hairs are soon lost, revealing green, which matures to brown beneath. Leaves and buds alternate. Buds are egg shaped and pointed, orange brown with white hairs.

Leaves (6-12 cm) are always silver white and woolly when young. The wool soon rubs off the upper surface leaving it a shiny, dark green, but remains greyish white on the underside. Shape is variable, with three to five triangular lobes with a few teeth. Base is rounded or a shallow heart-shape. Margin has no translucent strip, size from 6-12 cm. Leaf stalk is slightly flattened, woolly.

Male catkins appear in spring before the leaves. They are crimson, with grey wool, and expand to 8 cm.

Female catkins are green, expanding as the fruit ripens to 8-10 cm.

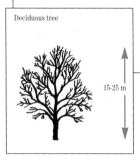

SIMILAR SPECIES
Populus canescens
Leaves of grey poplar are grey and hairy beneath when young, toothed but not lobed, except on the most vigorous shoots.

Deciduous tree

15-25 m

White poplar, also known as abele, is native to Europe from Portugal and Spain in the west, north through central France and Germany, and from there east into Central Asia; it is also native to coastal North Africa. It has been widely planted outside these areas, including in Britain, for its attractive, silvery foliage. As it suckers from the roots, plantings soon form clumps and appear to present natural stands. The natural habitat is fertile, well-drained but damp soils in full sun. Like other poplars, it does not tolerate shade, but, unlike most, it will not tolerate waterlogged sites. The timber is soft and white.

Grey poplar is a natural hybrid between white poplar and aspen, intermediate between the two parent species, but with hybrid vigour. It occurs where the two species grow together, but is also widely planted as a specimen tree. As with both parents, it suckers profusely and soon establishes a grove of saplings. The leaves are initially hairy, as in white poplar, but grey rather than vivid silver. Their shape, especially on the weaker shoots, is rounded as in aspen; only the most vigorous shoots produce strongly-lobed leaves.

134

The rounded, domed crown of white poplar is particularly attractive when the leaves are moved by the wind to reveal the vivid silver-white undersides. Illustrated here is an old tree growing beside the Yarlung Tsangpo in south-east Tibet.

BARK

Grey green or creamy white, smooth on young trees, with small black pits. It becomes black, cracked and furrowed at the base of old trees.

Goat willow

Salix caprea

Leaves are set alternately, egg shaped or oblong (broad end attached), 5-10 cm by 3-6 cm. Apex has a blunt or short point. Base is rounded. Margin has shallow, rounded or pointed teeth. Upper side is rough with impressed veins, underside has a grey bloom, soft down and raised veins. Leaf stalk (1 cm) is dark red.

SIMILAR SPECIES
Salix cinerea
Common sallow's leaves are egg shaped (broad end attached), 2-9 cm by 1-3 cm. Underside has reddish hairs.

Deciduous tree

6-12 m

Shoots are initially hairy and grey, maturing to reddish brown or yellow green. Bark stripped off one-year shoots reveals smooth wood. Buds, 0.4 cm, are egg shaped and pointed.

Catkins develop in late winter before the leaves. Males are silver in bud, but yellow when expanded to 3 cm, when they shed pollen. Females are pale green, maturing into 3-7-cm fruits in May-June.

Common sallow's shoot is more slender than that of goat willow, with straight ridges if bark is removed from second-year shoot.

Goat willow is native throughout Europe, except for the southern part of the Iberian peninsular and the far north and east into Asia. It usually makes a small tree, often on several stems, but it can be drawn to a tree of 20 m or so in woodland. The male trees furnish the 'pussy willow' catkins and are infinitely more attractive (furry and silver coloured) than the rather insipid female catkins, both as they open and as they expand to release their pollen. The fruit ripens in early summer and releases masses of small fluffy seeds which float on the lightest breeze. They are viable for only a couple of days and must land on bare, damp soil in order to germinate: so they don't survive unless there's a wet spell in early summer. After germination, the tree can grow on a wide range of sites.

Common sallow is similar in character and habit to goat willow, and they often occur together. Common sallow's narrower leaf (rusty and hairy underneath) is the best separator, but another useful difference is common sallow's ridges on the wood of the second-year shoots; in goat willow the shoots are smooth. This can only be seen if the bark is removed from a length of the shoot.

Goat willow is found on a wide range of sites, its main need being open damp soil in the vicinity when the seeds are released in July. It makes a dense leafy tree with a domed crown.

Bark is smooth and pale grey, developing orange fissures on older trees.

Violet willow

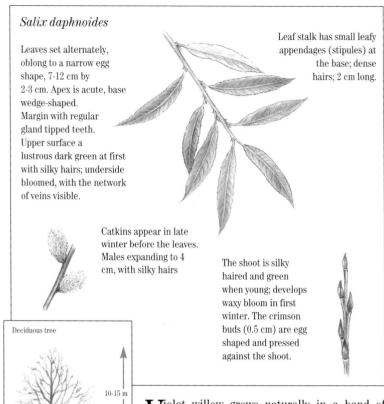

Salix daphnoides

Leaves set alternately, oblong to a narrow egg shape, 7-12 cm by 2-3 cm. Apex is acute, base wedge-shaped. Margin with regular gland tipped teeth. Upper surface a lustrous dark green at first with silky hairs; underside bloomed, with the network of veins visible.

Leaf stalk has small leafy appendages (stipules) at the base; dense hairs; 2 cm long.

Catkins appear in late winter before the leaves. Males expanding to 4 cm, with silky hairs

The shoot is silky haired and green when young; develops waxy bloom in first winter. The crimson buds (0.5 cm) are egg shaped and pressed against the shoot.

Deciduous tree

10-15 m

Violet willow grows naturally in a band of Central Europe from Italy and the Balkans north through eastern France to southern Scandinavia, and east to Finland and the western Ukraine. However, it is widely cultivated outside this area for its attractive foliage and the male catkins. It is also grown for the winter effect of the heavily bloomed shoots. This waxy bloom is washed off over time, but often persists beneath the buds. The effect can be heightened if the tree is cut down in the spring and allowed to coppice or to make strong new growths from the base. These may reach 2 m or more during the summer and are very waxy, can also be used as osiers to make baskets.

A closely related tree from Russia east into Central Asia is *S. acutifolia*, often treated as a subspecies. This has been planted to stabilize sand dunes. It has similar, if less intense, waxy covering of the shoots, but is more attractive during summer with its narrower leaves set on twigs that hang down more than violet willow's. The leaves have around 15 pairs of veins, while in violet willow there are eight to 12 pairs of veins.

Violet willow is native to the banks of streams and to chalky gravel sites. It forms a conical or spiky crown in young trees, becoming rounded with age.

BARK
Smooth and grey, but on older trees it fissures at the base.

White willow

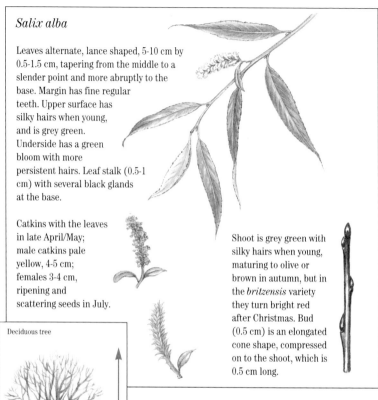

Salix alba

Leaves alternate, lance shaped, 5-10 cm by 0.5-1.5 cm, tapering from the middle to a slender point and more abruptly to the base. Margin has fine regular teeth. Upper surface has silky hairs when young, and is grey green. Underside has a green bloom with more persistent hairs. Leaf stalk (0.5-1 cm) with several black glands at the base.

Catkins with the leaves in late April/May; male catkins pale yellow, 4-5 cm; females 3-4 cm, ripening and scattering seeds in July.

Shoot is grey green with silky hairs when young, maturing to olive or brown in autumn, but in the *britzensis* variety they turn bright red after Christmas. Bud (0.5 cm) is an elongated cone shape, compressed on to the shoot, which is 0.5 cm long.

Deciduous tree

10-30 m

This species is native from southern England across Europe and into Central Asia. It thrives on damp sites which may be flooded from time to time; or it grows beside streams and rivers, with other species which like a damp situation. However, it also grows happily on less damp sites if planted, though it won't regenerate naturally on these sites. The timber is soft and light, yet also springy and withstands shocks. The most famous form of white willow is var. *caerulea*, – the 'cricket bat' willow. This is a selected fast-growing form, which is planted as 'setts' – large unrooted cuttings put down in damp sites at 8-m spacings. The lowest 4-5 m of the trunk is kept free of branches and is harvested after 15 years. The trunks are cut into lengths of about 0.7 m and split to give the triangular blanks which are then shaped into bats.

Two other varieties are *britzensis* whose red twigs lighten up the country-side after Christmas – it is particularly effective in February sun and can be grown as a coppiced shrub; and *argentea* which has many more silky hairs on the leaves, making a silvery-grey tree.

White willow is commonly found growing along river banks, where it forms an attractive tree with its dense, leafy crown. This is conical in young trees and rounded or domed in old ones.

BARK
Grey brown, becoming deeply fissured and ridged.

Crack willow

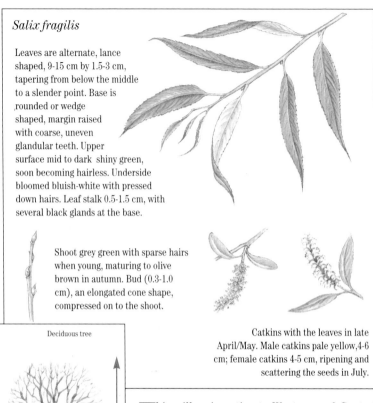

Salix fragilis

Leaves are alternate, lance shaped, 9-15 cm by 1.5-3 cm, tapering from below the middle to a slender point. Base is rounded or wedge shaped, margin raised with coarse, uneven glandular teeth. Upper surface mid to dark shiny green, soon becoming hairless. Underside bloomed bluish-white with pressed down hairs. Leaf stalk 0.5-1.5 cm, with several black glands at the base.

Shoot grey green with sparse hairs when young, maturing to olive brown in autumn. Bud (0.3-1.0 cm), an elongated cone shape, compressed on to the shoot.

Deciduous tree

10-20 m

Catkins with the leaves in late April/May. Male catkins pale yellow, 4-6 cm; female catkins 4-5 cm, ripening and scattering the seeds in July.

This willow is native to Western and Central Europe from Norway and Britain south to Spain and across to Romania. It makes a smaller tree than the closely related white willow (page 140) from which it can be distinguished by the much less hairy and generally larger leaves which are glossy above and taper from below the middle.

The name crack willow (and the scientific name *fragilis*, which translates as fragile) refer to the way in which second-year twigs will snap with a clear but staggered break on only a very light backward pressure. White willow twigs will also snap, but not as easily and without such a clean break. Twigs older than two years do not snap easily, neither do the current year's twigs until they have ripened. The snapped twigs will root if they land on suitably damp soil, and establish a forest of saplings. Crack and white willows are frequently grown as pollards along river banks. These are formed by cutting the trunk off at 3 m. The resulting new growths (out of reach of horses and cattle) were harvested for small timber or cut for winter fodder.

The crown of crack willow is rounded (as shown here) if a tree has grown in the open. Young trees are spiky and conical; older ones are more ragged because they lose branches in strong winds.

BARK
Grey, scaly when young and developing coarse, deep fissures with thick ridges when mature.

Weeping willow

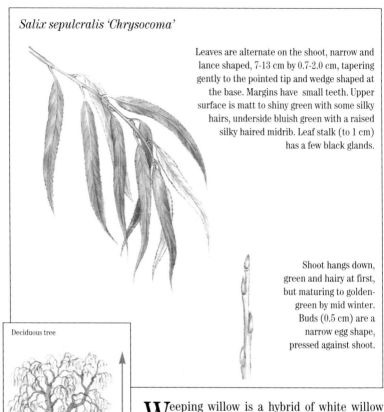

Salix sepulcralis 'Chrysocoma'

Leaves are alternate on the shoot, narrow and lance shaped, 7-13 cm by 0.7-2.0 cm, tapering gently to the pointed tip and wedge shaped at the base. Margins have small teeth. Upper surface is matt to shiny green with some silky hairs, underside bluish green with a raised silky haired midrib. Leaf stalk (to 1 cm) has a few black glands.

Shoot hangs down, green and hairy at first, but maturing to golden-green by mid winter. Buds (0.5 cm) are a narrow egg shape, pressed against shoot.

Deciduous tree

10-18 m

Weeping willow is a hybrid of white willow (page 140) and the Chinese weeping willow, *Salix babylonica* (see below). The commonest form is the cultivar 'Chrysocoma' which has a golden-twigged form of white willow as one parent. With its golden twigs and vigorous weeping habit, this has supplanted other forms of weeping willow. Like most willows, 'Chrysocoma' roots readily from cuttings and is propagated commercially from hardwood cuttings taken in late winter and stuck into the ground. However, a twig broken off in mid winter will root if placed in water on a window cill, with the white roots erupting after a week or so from the stem just beneath the water's surface.

Salix babylonica, a Chinese species, is the tree illustrated on the 'willow' pattern of china. It was given the scientific name *babylonica* because it was originally identified as the willow in Psalm 137, verse 2. However, this is now believed to be an incorrect translation, as the trees referred to in the psalm were, in fact, poplars. *Salix babylonica* can be distinguished by the green or brownish-green shoots and the long, slender twisted tip of the leaves.

144

Weeping willow is very graceful when growing beside a lake or river with its branches hanging over the water and reflected in it.

BARK
Golden green and smooth on young trees. After several years it turns brown and develops coarse ridges and fissures.

145

Bay willow

Salix pentandra

Flowers appear in May-June on short leafy side shoots. Male catkins are cylindrical, yellow, 2-8 cm.

Leaves are alternate, variable in shape from egg shaped (broad end attached) to a broad lance shape, 5-12 cm by 2-5 cm. Apex has a slender point, base is rounded to wedge shaped. Margin has fine, glandular teeth. Upper surface is glossy dark green, underside paler, without hairs. Leaf stalk (1 cm), has several glands near the blade.

Shoot is glossy olive green when young, but maturing to brown or red by autumn.

Fruit ripens in July, capsules 1 cm.

Deciduous tree

10-20 m

This willow is a tree of cooler regions. In Britain it is confined to the north of England, North Wales, Ireland and Scotland. It occurs across Northern and Central Europe and east into Asia, with scattered populations further south only on high mountain chains. It is an attractive tree, particular for the lustrous foliage which has a passing resemblance to the leaves of the bay laurel (page 283) and for the catkins. These are carried on leafy shoots in late spring. As is usual with willows, the male catkins are larger and more showy than the female flowers. The scientific name refers to the five stamens of the male catkins.

Willows are very closely related to poplars and both generally have separate male and female trees. They differ in two major respects. Willows are pollinated by bees and other insects, whereas poplars are wind pollinated. In willows there is no terminal bud on a shoot, and the shoot tip falls off when extension growth ceases – next year's extension growth is made from a side bud. In poplars, the growing cells at the shoot tip form a bud which makes next year's extension growth.

Bay willow develops a rounded or domed crown. In female trees (as in this photograph), the fluffy fruits can make a show in July.

BARK
Grey or grey brown, developing shallow orange fissures.

Oak or pedunculate oak

Quercus robur
Shoot matures to shiny grey green; buds egg shaped and bluntly pointed. Leaves are alternate along the shoots, but clustered towards the tips. They are stiff or card-like in texture, 4-12 cm by 2-6 cm, broadest in upper two thirds. Apex is rounded. Narrow towards the base, which has two ear-like lobes. Margin has four to six large, rounded lobes and rounded indentations or spaces between them. Leaf stalk is 0.4-0.7 cm, rarely as long as 1 cm.

Leaf matt green on upper side, but often covered by honeydew. Underside is pale, waxy bluish green with raised veins.

Male catkins (2-4 cm) hanging with the new leaves in spring. One to four acorns set on a long slender stalk (2-10 cm), ripening in first autumn,. They are egg shaped to oblong, 1.5-4 cm, set in a cup which encloses the lower quarter.

SIMILAR SPECIES
Quercus frainetto
Leaves of Hungarian oak are larger than oak's, 10-25 cm by 6-14 cm, with a wedge-shaped or slightly ear-like base and about nine pairs of lobes, largest when the leaf is broadest.

Deciduous tree

15-35 m

Oak is known as English oak and pedunculate oak, from the long stalk or peduncle which carries the acorns. This familiar tree is native throughout Europe, except the far north, and extends to the east into the Caucasus. In Britain it is commonest in the drier south and east, with most of the oaks in the wetter north and west being the related sessile oak. Exceptions to this rule include Dartmoor, where the highest oak woods are sessile.

Oak has an excellent timber, which is hard and durable, with an attractive grain. Its appearance is the result of the variation between the less dense spring wood (formed when the tree is growing rapidly in spring and requiring large water vessels to transport water) and the much denser wood formed in summer (when growth is slowed and the tree can make wood that gives strength to the trunk and branches). In oak, the ray cells which transport material between different growth rings, are larger and more prominent than in most timbers. Hungarian oak is native to southern Italy and the Balkans. It is distinctive for its large leaves with deep lobes see above.

Oak is of course a familiar tree of lowland woods and hedgerows; not so well known is that it does very well on heavy clay soils – in fact it tolerates a range of sites. Old trees in the open develop broad, rounded crowns, but in woodland the trees quickly loose their lower branches.

BARK
In young trees smooth, grey green and shiny, becoming increasingly fissured. On old trees it is grey brown, ridged and furrowed.

149

Sessile oak

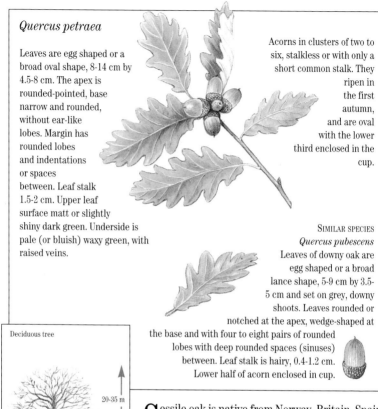

Quercus petraea

Leaves are egg shaped or a broad oval shape, 8-14 cm by 4.5-8 cm. The apex is rounded-pointed, base narrow and rounded, without ear-like lobes. Margin has rounded lobes and indentations or spaces between. Leaf stalk 1.5-2 cm. Upper leaf surface matt or slightly shiny dark green. Underside is pale (or bluish) waxy green, with raised veins.

Acorns in clusters of two to six, stalkless or with only a short common stalk. They ripen in the first autumn, and are oval with the lower third enclosed in the cup.

SIMILAR SPECIES
Quercus pubescens
Leaves of downy oak are egg shaped or a broad lance shape, 5-9 cm by 3.5-5 cm and set on grey, downy shoots. Leaves rounded or notched at the apex, wedge-shaped at the base and with four to eight pairs of rounded lobes with deep rounded spaces (sinuses) between. Leaf stalk is hairy, 0.4-1.2 cm. Lower half of acorn enclosed in cup.

Deciduous tree

20-35 m

Sessile oak is native from Norway, Britain, Spain and Portugal east across Europe to Poland, south-western Russia, the Crimea and into northern Greece. It does not occur in southern Italy, where it is replaced by closely related species. Its timber is similar to pedunculate oak's (page 148), but it tends to make a better forest tree, with a longer straight trunk. In England it is commonest on light, wet soils, being less frequent than pedunculate oak on heavy clay soils. The two species can be separated by sessile oak's more regular lobes, narrow rounded leaf on a long stalk and the acorns either stalk-less or short-stalked. Pedunculate oak's acorns are on a long stalk or peduncle, the leaves are less neatly lobed and have auricles or ear-like lobes at the base with only a short leaf stalk. Occasionally, the two species hybridize. The name sessile oak comes from the stalk to the acorns, not the leaves. It is also known as durmast oak.

Downy oak, also called white oak, is native to the region from western France and northern Spain east across southern Europe to Turkey and the Caucasus. It is commonly found on sunny limestone or silty soils.

Sessile oak makes the best stands of timber when close grown, but in the open (as shown here) it forms a wide, spreading tree.

BARK
Grey brown and smooth on young trees, becoming finely fissured and cracked into ridges and furrows on old trees.

Holm oak

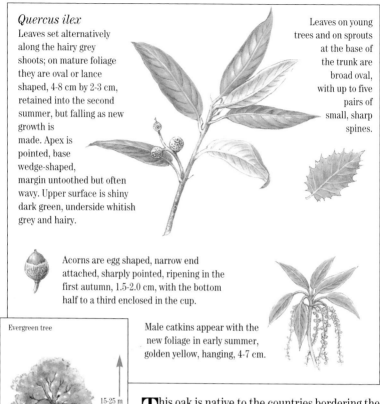

Quercus ilex
Leaves set alternatively along the hairy grey shoots; on mature foliage they are oval or lance shaped, 4-8 cm by 2-3 cm, retained into the second summer, but falling as new growth is made. Apex is pointed, base wedge-shaped, margin untoothed but often wavy. Upper surface is shiny dark green, underside whitish grey and hairy.

Leaves on young trees and on sprouts at the base of the trunk are broad oval, with up to five pairs of small, sharp spines.

Acorns are egg shaped, narrow end attached, sharply pointed, ripening in the first autumn, 1.5-2.0 cm, with the bottom half to a third enclosed in the cup.

Evergreen tree

15-25 m

Male catkins appear with the new foliage in early summer, golden yellow, hanging, 4-7 cm.

This oak is native to the countries bordering the Mediterranean and the southern Black Sea, but is absent from the Egyptian and Israeli coasts. It is very tolerant of hot, dry sites and coastal exposure. The species is becoming naturalized in southern England and is expected to become much commoner as a result of global warming. It is planted as an evergreen, but looks dull for 11 months of the year and really should (like copper beeches and other trees with heavy, dull foliage) only be permitted under licence. The leaves fall in early summer, to the annoyance of tidy gardeners. It casts a dense shade and the roots dry the soil, preventing other plants growing beneath it, even spring bulbs. There are much more attractive evergreen trees. The wood is dense, not easily worked, best for fuel and charcoal.

The specific name *ilex* is from the Latin name for the tree. This name is now used as the generic name for hollies (page 216). With holly, it shares a tendency to have untoothed leaves on mature trees, but spiny leaves on juvenile plants and on sprouts at the base of older trees.

Dark and sombre for much of the year, holm oak bursts into life with new foliage and its golden yellow catkins in early summer. The crown is rounded and frequently may extend down to ground level.

BARK
Smooth on young trees, black or dark brown, becoming cracked into small, thin curling squares.

Turkey oak

Quercus cerris

Leaves set alternately along the shoots. They are oblong to egg shaped but variously lobed, with deep, scalloped sinuses, 5-14 cm by 3.5-6cm. Apex is rounded, base rounded or cut off, lobes often ending in a small point. Upper surface is a deep green and rough to the touch, underside has a dense covering of whitish hairs and six to ten pairs of raised veins. Leaf stalk 1-2 cm long.

Shoot hairy, grey-brown, with egg-shaped pointed buds surrounded by long, wispy, coarse hairs.

Acorns ripen over two summers. First--year acorns are small, in the axils of leaves on weaker shoots, expanding in the second year and ripening to 1.5-2.2 cm. Cup encloses lower third of acorn and has many straight, mossy scales. These are reflexed at the base of the cup, but at the top they point forwards.

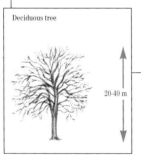

Deciduous tree

20-40 m

Turkey oak is native to Southern Europe from south-eastern France to Turkey and north into the Czech Republic and Romania. As a young tree, it quickly makes a narrow conical- or column-shaped crown. When it emerges from the canopy of other trees and has light on all sides, it develops a wide, spreading crown and can cover a quarter of an acre (¹/₁₀ th of a hectare). It grows faster in Britain than pedunculate and sessile oaks (pages 148 and 150), but the timber is poor, lacking the rays which give these two species their hardness and durability. The bark is rich in tannins and can be used to tan leather – the tannins soften the leather and prevent it rotting. The tree can be identified during the winter period when leafless by the wispy scales around all the buds. This feature is unique to Turkey oak (some oaks from south-eastern Europe have similar scales around the terminal cluster of buds only). Turkey oak grows well on all soils. Unlike pedunculate and sessile oak, it does not respond well to being pollarded (which allows really old trees with stout trunks but small crowns to develop) and rarely lasts more than a couple of centuries.

Turkey oak forms a large and wide-spreading tree, especially common in parks and large gardens. Young trees may retain their brown autumn leaves over winter.

BARK
Grey to silvery grey, quickly becoming fissured and developing hard, corky ridges.

Cork oak

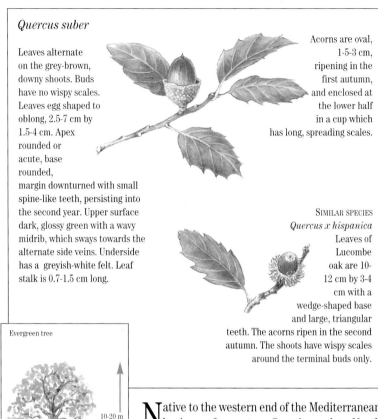

Quercus suber

Leaves alternate on the grey-brown, downy shoots. Buds have no wispy scales. Leaves egg shaped to oblong, 2.5-7 cm by 1.5-4 cm. Apex rounded or acute, base rounded, margin downturned with small spine-like teeth, persisting into the second year. Upper surface dark, glossy green with a wavy midrib, which sways towards the alternate side veins. Underside has a greyish-white felt. Leaf stalk is 0.7-1.5 cm long.

Acorns are oval, 1.5-3 cm, ripening in the first autumn, and enclosed at the lower half in a cup which has long, spreading scales.

Similar species
Quercus x hispanica
Leaves of Lucombe oak are 10-12 cm by 3-4 cm with a wedge-shaped base and large, triangular teeth. The acorns ripen in the second autumn. The shoots have wispy scales around the terminal buds only.

Evergreen tree

10-20 m

Native to the western end of the Mediterranean basin, as far east as Croatia, and to North Africa in Morocco, cork oak is also an important tree in Spain and Portugal, where the outer bark is harvested for cork. Young trees are first ready for harvesting when they are about 20 to 25 years old, although the first cut does not produce the best bark. Later harvestings are on seven- to ten-year cycles. Care must be taken not to damage the inner bark, or the tree will be harmed. The bark is used for stopping wine bottles and as a decorative and insulating material. The continued harvesting of cork ensures both the survival of the tree and the wide range of wildlife which relies upon it – a *status quo* threatened by wine producers who use plastic stoppers.

Lucombe oak is a natural hybrid between cork oak and Turkey oak, found where the two species meet in south-eastern France and Italy, and also wherever the two species are grown together. It is variable between the parents, some forms having so corky bark, but most having hard bark. It tends to be semi-evergreen, losing its leaves in cold periods after Christmas.

Cork oak develops a rounded crown, which is usually broader than high when grown in the open.

BARK
Top layer corky and grey brown, developing deep fissures and ridges; under layer red brown or pink.

Red oak

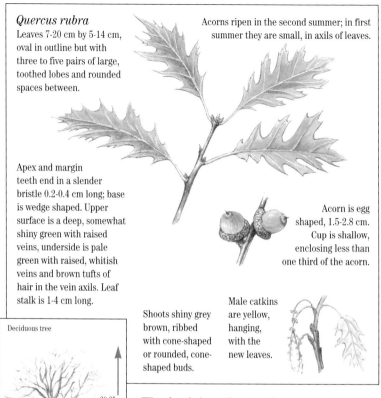

Quercus rubra
Leaves 7-20 cm by 5-14 cm, oval in outline but with three to five pairs of large, toothed lobes and rounded spaces between.

Acorns ripen in the second summer; in first summer they are small, in axils of leaves.

Apex and margin teeth end in a slender bristle 0.2-0.4 cm long; base is wedge shaped. Upper surface is a deep, somewhat shiny green with raised veins, underside is pale green with raised, whitish veins and brown tufts of hair in the vein axils. Leaf stalk is 1-4 cm long.

Acorn is egg shaped, 1.5-2.8 cm. Cup is shallow, enclosing less than one third of the acorn.

Shoots shiny grey brown, ribbed with cone-shaped or rounded, cone-shaped buds.

Male catkins are yellow, hanging, with the new leaves.

Deciduous tree

20-25 m

Red oak is native to a large area of eastern North America from the southern side of the St. Lawrence River west to Minnesota and south to Oklahoma and Georgia. It is the commonest of the American oaks in cultivation in Britain and Europe, and forms a large tree. It is also grown to some extent in forestry, as it has a useful timber, is a faster grower than pedunculate oak (page 148) and does well on acidic sands. However, it does not thrive on shallow soils over chalk. The main branches radiate out from the trunk. The foliage often turns an impressive red in autumn, covering the entire cown at the same time. This gives rise to both the common and scientific names, but some trees make nothing better than a poor brown – if buying one from a nursery, make your choice when the tree is in autumn colour in order to select the best. The new foliage in spring is yellow for several days.

Red oak is a member of an entirely American section of the genus, characterized by the bristle-like tips to the teeth or side lobes of the leaves. (The bristles are made by the veins extending beyond the end of the leaf.)

Red oak forms a tall, wide tree with big, spreading branches. The crown is more open than on other oaks and allows dappled sunlight to penetrate to the forest floor.

BARK
Silvery grey or dark grey and smooth in young trees, developing scaly ridges in old trees and showing the red inner bark in the fissures.

Scarlet oak

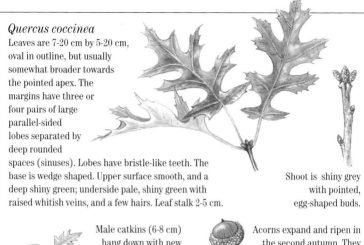

Quercus coccinea
Leaves are 7-20 cm by 5-20 cm, oval in outline, but usually somewhat broader towards the pointed apex. The margins have three or four pairs of large parallel-sided lobes separated by deep rounded spaces (sinuses). Lobes have bristle-like teeth. The base is wedge shaped. Upper surface smooth, and a deep shiny green; underside pale, shiny green with raised whitish veins, and a few hairs. Leaf stalk 2-5 cm.

Shoot is shiny grey with pointed, egg-shaped buds.

Male catkins (6-8 cm) hang down with new foliage in spring. Female flowers on short shoots in leaf axils.

Acorns expand and ripen in the second autumn. They are egg shaped, 1.2-2.5 cm, and sit in an open cup which encloses the lower third to a half.

SIMILAR SPECIES
Quercus palustris
Leaves of pin oak smaller than scarlet oak's, with the middle pair of lobes spread wider. There are hairs on the upperside veins, and especially in the vein axils beneath (where they are fawn-coloured tufts).

Deciduous tree

20-30 m

Scarlet oak is native to eastern North America from Maine south to Georgia and west to Mississippi and Indiana, where it is found in forests on poor soils. It is the second commonest American oak in cultivation in Europe after red oak (page 158), and, like the red oak, its leaf veins extend beyond the end of the leaf blade as slender filaments. However, it is most easily separated from red oak by the deep and regular spaces (sinuses) between the leaf lobes and the almost hairless, shinier leaves. The branch structure does not have the heavy radiating main branches of red oak, but tends to be more upright, with more twigs in the crown. Both the common name and scientific name refer to the scarlet autumn colour.

Pin oak, *Quercus palustris*, is native to eastern North America from Vermont across to southern Ontario and Iowa south to Oklahoma and South Carolina, where it occurs in marshy sites (the scientific name means marshy). The acorn is nearly round and sits on a saucer-shaped cup enclosing the lower third to a quarter. The crown's lower branches hang down.

Brilliant in autumn colour, scarlet oak forms a large tree 'with a tall, domed crown. The branch structure lacks the heavy, radiating main branches of red oak (page 158) and the tree tends to be more upright, with a twiggy crown.

BARK
Silver grey to dark grey, smooth but with warts. As the tree matures it becomes fissured into fine, scaly ridges revealing the red inner bark.

Sweet chestnut

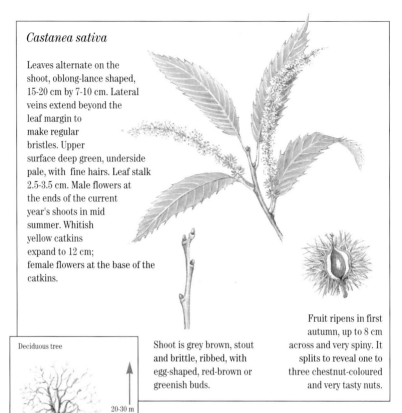

Castanea sativa

Leaves alternate on the shoot, oblong-lance shaped, 15-20 cm by 7-10 cm. Lateral veins extend beyond the leaf margin to make regular bristles. Upper surface deep green, underside pale, with fine hairs. Leaf stalk 2.5-3.5 cm. Male flowers at the ends of the current year's shoots in mid summer. Whitish yellow catkins expand to 12 cm; female flowers at the base of the catkins.

Deciduous tree

20-30 m

Shoot is grey brown, stout and brittle, ribbed, with egg-shaped, red-brown or greenish buds.

Fruit ripens in first autumn, up to 8 cm across and very spiny. It splits to reveal one to three chestnut-coloured and very tasty nuts.

Also known as Spanish chestnut, sweet chestnut is native across southern Europe from Spain to Turkey and east into the Caucasus. In North Africa it occurs in Tunisia. It is one of the trees which is likely to benefit in Britain from global warming: it is happiest on sites which are hot and dry during the summer. It is particularly at home on acidic, sandy and gravelly sites, and not well adapted to chalky soils. It does not tolerate waterlogging at the roots and on such soils is likely to be killed or damaged by *Phytophthora*, a small yeast-like fungus. It is also threatened by the fungus *Endothia*; this is native to eastern Asia, but has been introduced into Europe. It has almost exterminated the closely-related American sweet chestnut which once formed extensive forests.

The timber is similar to pedunculate oak, but without the large rays which give character to oak wood. The tree regrows readily when cut down and the resulting stems are harvested on a ten to 15 year cycle for poles and pales. The pales are split to make chestnut pale fencing. The best bit of the tree, however, is the nut: delicious when roasted – and they make excellent stuffing.

Old sweet chestnuts, with their tall, domed crowns, can make attractive trees, although they often have a few suckers at their feet. Young trees are much more column shaped, with rather whorled branching.

BARK
Smooth and shiny grey on young trees, later developing fissures and ridges, which often spiral up the trunk.

Beech

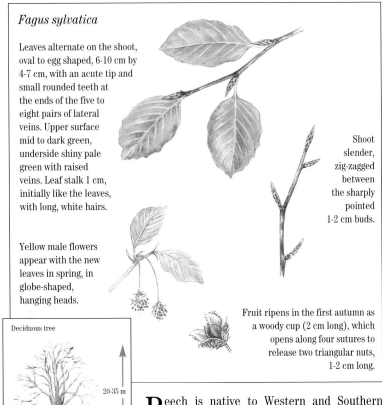

Fagus sylvatica

Leaves alternate on the shoot, oval to egg shaped, 6-10 cm by 4-7 cm, with an acute tip and small rounded teeth at the ends of the five to eight pairs of lateral veins. Upper surface mid to dark green, underside shiny pale green with raised veins. Leaf stalk 1 cm, initially like the leaves, with long, white hairs.

Shoot slender, zig-zagged between the sharply pointed 1-2 cm buds.

Yellow male flowers appear with the new leaves in spring, in globe-shaped, hanging heads.

Deciduous tree

20-35 m

Fruit ripens in the first autumn as a woody cup (2 cm long), which opens along four sutures to release two triangular nuts, 1-2 cm long.

Beech is native to Western and Southern Europe, from the Balkans and the Ukraine to the Pyrenees, south-eastern England and southern Sweden. Like sweet chestnut (page 162), it does not grow well on waterlogged or clay soils, preferring well-drained places whether they are acidic or alkaline. It is, however, shallow rooting and needs cool and moist conditions at the roots. Over much of Europe it occurs with *Abies alba* (page 70). The timber is excellent, easily worked, and used for furniture and dowels. Beech casts a dense shade resulting in open, airy woods, ideal for walking through, but not for wildlife. The new foliage in spring is an exquisite light green; autumn brings a beautiful russet colour. However, a major failing of the species is its readiness to provide trees with an excess of purple xanthocyanin. This masks the chlorophyll which gives most trees their pleasing green colour. Some people plant these dull copper-coloured trees to excess – admittedly they can be attractive for a few short weeks in spring, but is that really a price worth paying for their washed-out appearance for the rest of the summer?

Beech makes attractive specimen trees as well as forming extensive forests. The rounded crown is very dense in healthy trees; in less healthy ones, the twigs are bunched, with spaces between the smaller branches. Shown here is a tree in autumn.

BARK
Smooth and silvery grey throughout the life of most trees, although some occasionally become scaly at the base.

Wych elm

Ulmus glabra

Leaves oval to elongated oval, 8-18 cm by 4-10 cm. Apex slender and pointed, often with a broad shoulder, or with three (or more) large, triangular lobes. Margin has coarse double teeth. Base is very oblique – markedly different on the two sides. Upper surface very rough with 14-20 pairs of impressed veins, underside hairy with raised veins. Leaf stalk less than 0.6 cm.

Purplish-red flowers appear before the leaves in late winter.

Shoot brown and stout, but often zig-zagged, with pointed chocolate-brown buds, 0.6-0.8 cm long.

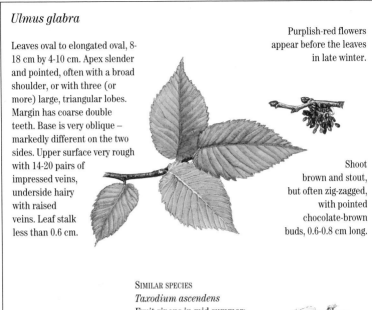

SIMILAR SPECIES
Taxodium ascendens
Fruit ripens in mid summer: flattened discs (2.5 cm) with a central seed and a notched tip, carried in dense clusters. It is light green before ripening brown.

Deciduous tree

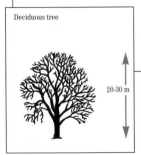

20-30 m

Native to most of Europe except the far north and most of Spain and Portugal, wych elm also occurs in parts of Turkey. Throughout most of its range, the leaves have lobes or large teeth on the shoulders, but these are absent on the trees from northern Britain and Scandinavia.

This is the only elm which is clearly native to Britain and the only one which reproduces entirely from seed, unlike English elm and smooth-leaved elm, which rely upon root suckers. Wych elm has a reasonable timber, once used for coffins and furniture, but the devastation caused by Dutch elm disease has made the timber less readily available. Another historical use for the timber was to make water pipes – the wood lasts indefinitely if kept wet and wych elm pipes survive from Roman times.

The scientific name, *glabra,* translates as smooth and is often used in the sense of hairless. The leaves of wych elm, however, are rough to the touch and hairy on the underside. The smoothness in this case refers to the bark, which remains so, at least for several years.

The rounded, domed crown is enhanced in late winter by the purplish male flowers, and in autumn by an attractive yellow.

BARK
Smooth and silvery grey for a number of years, then becoming grey brown and fissured with interconnecting ridges.

Huntingdon elm or Dutch elm

Ulmus hollandica

Leaves alternate on the shoot, 10-15 cm by 5-8 cm, oval or egg shaped. Apex has an abrupt, short slender point. Base uneven, rounded or heart shaped on one side and wedge shaped on the other. Margin has double teeth. Upper surface smooth and shiny green, underside pale with raised hairy veins. Leaf stalk stout and hairy, 1-2 cm long.

Shoot is brown, at first with long white hairs, but hairless by autumn, with egg-shaped shiny red-brown buds, up to 1 cm long.

Fruit (2 cm) ripens in late spring. Wing is notched.

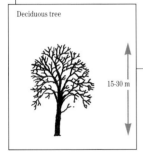

Deciduous tree

15-30 m

This tree is a hybrid between wych elm (page 166) and smooth-leaved elm (page 170). In the wild these two species occupy different habitats and probably only rarely crossed. However, both parent trees have been grown in parks and widely planted in their native areas for several centuries. The hybrid grows faster than either parent, quickly forming large trees. It is especially common in eastern England and the Low Countries (Belgium and The Netherlands). The Huntingdon elm (illustrated opposite) is a good form which arose in the middle of the 18th century. As is well known, *Ulmus hollandica*, like other elms, is susceptible to Dutch elm disease. This fungal disease blocks the water conducting vessels in the tree's wood, causing the death of the affected portions. The disease is usually progressive and can quickly kill entire trees. It is spread by a bark beetle, which breeds in the bark of newly dead trees or branches. When the beetles emerge in spring they fly off and feed on healthy trees, introducing the fungus. It is called Dutch elm disease because of the early research work carried out on the problem by Dutch scientists in the 1920s and 1930s.

Ulmus hollandica occurs in a number of forms but one of the most impressive is 'Vegeta', the Huntingdon elm shown here in Harrogate, Yorkshire.

BARK
Grey brown, smooth in young trees but becoming fissured into ridges or small scaly plates in old trees.

Smooth-leaved elm

Ulmus minor

Flowers in early spring, purplish-red. Fruit 1.2-1.5 cm, ripening in early summer.

Shoot glossy brown and hairy at first, later grey brown, with small (0.2-0.4 cm), dark shiny red buds. Leaves alternate on the shoot, 4-12 cm by 2.5-5 cm, oval, or egg shaped, apex a slender point. Base uneven, rounded on one side and wedge shaped on the other. Margin has double teeth. Upper surface smooth and shiny green, underside pale with ten to 13 pairs of raised hairy veins. Leaf stalk 0.5 cm and hairy.

SIMILAR SPECIES

Ulmus procera

English elm's leaves are a rounded egg-shap, sometimes oval, 4-10 cm by 3.5-7 cm. Margins have coarse double teeth. The upper surface is rough. The shoot is more slender than smooth-leaved elm's and persistently hairy, often developing corky wings.

Deciduous tree

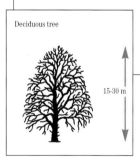

15-30 m

Smooth-leaved elm is native across Europe from Britain in the west, eastwards into western Asia. It also occurs in North Africa. There are several different forms across this range. These were probably used as tribal markers as our early ancestors migrated. Although elms have a useful timber, in past times they were managed mainly to provide fodder for cattle. Trees were lopped and the foliage either fed to the livestock during the periods of drought when there was little grass, or dried and kept for the winter.

English elm probably originated as a hybrid of smooth-leaved elm and is only common in England. It is best identified by the rough upper surface of the leaves. It does not produce viable seed, but spreads entirely by root suckers (unlike smooth-leaved elm, which spreads both by seed and by suckers, and wych elm, which spreads entirely by seed). It makes an attractive, tall domed crown and quickly forms a large volume of timber. It was much planted during the enclosures of Common Land in the 17th century, and then spread. Recently, it has been devastated by Dutch elm disease.

Smooth-leaved elm makes a neat tree with its glossy foliage. The many small leaves give a dense, leafy appearance to the conical or tall,-domed crown.

BARK
Silvery grey and smooth, becoming deeply fissured and ridged.

Fluttering elm

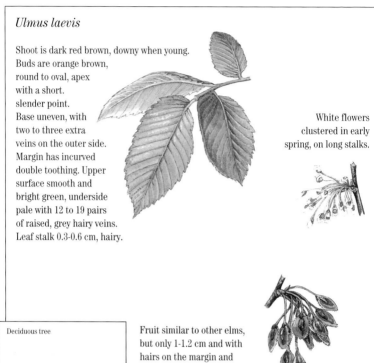

Ulmus laevis

Shoot is dark red brown, downy when young. Buds are orange brown, round to oval, apex with a short. slender point. Base uneven, with two to three extra veins on the outer side. Margin has incurved double toothing. Upper surface smooth and bright green, underside pale with 12 to 19 pairs of raised, grey hairy veins. Leaf stalk 0.3-0.6 cm, hairy.

White flowers clustered in early spring, on long stalks.

Deciduous tree

15-35 m

Fruit similar to other elms, but only 1-1.2 cm and with hairs on the margin and set on long stalks.

This elm, also known as European white elm, is native to Europe from the Pyrenees and north-eastern France and Belgium north to southern Finland; also east across to the Balkans and southern Russia and into Turkey and the Caucasus. It is one of the European trees which did not cross into Britain before the English Channel was flooded. It shows some tolerance of Dutch elm disease, but although planted in a few collections, it is rare in Britain.

The name fluttering elm arises from the long stalks or pedicels to the flowers and fruits, which allow the fruit to flutter in the slightest breeze. The alternative name of European white elm refers to the pale flowers. The scientific name *laevis* means smooth and is similar to the scientific name (*glabra*) of wych elm. However, in this instance it does refer to the leaves' upper surface.

This elm does not sucker freely, but reproduces by seed. As with other elms, these fall to the ground in early summer. They either germinate quickly if conditions are suitable, or die. The wood is hard and tough like that of other elms, but to some extent lacks their attractive grain.

172

Fluttering elm is a tree of lowland river valleys. The arching branches are characteristic of the winter silhouette and in summer carry massed foliage to give a billowing crown.

BARK
Grey brown and smooth in young trees, developing deep furrows with broad ridges in old trees.

Keaki

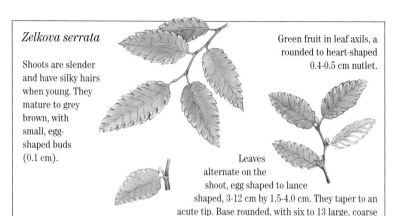

Zelkova serrata

Shoots are slender and have silky hairs when young. They mature to grey brown, with small, egg-shaped buds (0.1 cm).

Green fruit in leaf axils, a rounded to heart-shaped 0.4-0.5 cm nutlet.

Leaves alternate on the shoot, egg shaped to lance shaped, 3-12 cm by 1.5-4.0 cm. They taper to an acute tip. Base rounded, with six to 13 large, coarse triangular teeth. Dark green above, paler beneath and hairy on both sides: leaf stalk round, 0.7 cm.

SIMILAR SPECIES
Zelkova carpinifolia
Caucasian elm's leaves are oblong, 3-9 cm by 1.5-4.0 cm, usually rounded at the tip and at the base, which is uneven - see illustration. The margins have rounded teeth with a small abrupt point. Side veins fork, with one side running to the point and the other to the sinus or space between the teeth.

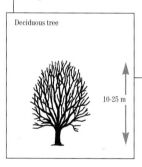

Deciduous tree

10-25 m

Fruit of Caucasian elm is egg-shaped, ribbed, 0.5-0.6 cm.

Keaki is native to the southern part of Japan, to Taiwan and to mainland Asia in Korea and north-east China. It can make a large tree, but is most often seen in recent plantings where it is rather flat topped and broader than high. It is only grown in Europe as an ornamental. Keaki is the Japanese name.

Caucasian elm is native from eastern Turkey to Armenia and Georgia, and to northern Iran on the southern side of the Caspian Sea. It makes an erect growing tree with many ascending stems arranged like the pipes of an organ. Formerly it was much commoner than Keaki and makes a larger tree. However, most of the old trees were killed at the height of the 1970s epidemic of Dutch elm disease. Generally, it is not particularly susceptible to the disease, but in the mid 1970s the population of elm bark beetles was so large and the surviving elms so few that hunger overcame their disinclination for *Zelkova*. The scientific name refers to the similarity of the leaves to hornbeam.

The two species can easily be separated by the rounded teeth of *carpinifolia,* as opposed to the triangular teeth of *serrata.*

174

Keaki makes a spreading, small tree, green and leafy during summer and a mixture of yellow, orange and pink in autumn.

BARK
Smooth and grey with prominent pink, orange or brown breathing pores (lenticels).

Nettle tree

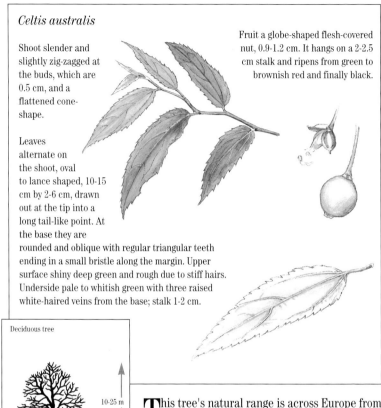

Celtis australis

Shoot slender and slightly zig-zagged at the buds, which are 0.5 cm, and a flattened cone-shape.

Leaves alternate on the shoot, oval to lance shaped, 10-15 cm by 2-6 cm, drawn out at the tip into a long tail-like point. At the base they are rounded and oblique with regular triangular teeth ending in a small bristle along the margin. Upper surface shiny deep green and rough due to stiff hairs. Underside pale to whitish green with three raised white-haired veins from the base; stalk 1-2 cm.

Fruit a globe-shaped flesh-covered nut, 0.9-1.2 cm. It hangs on a 2-2.5 cm stalk and ripens from green to brownish red and finally black.

Deciduous tree

10-25 m

This tree's natural range is across Europe from Portugal and Spain through southern France, Italy and the Balkans to Turkey, but never far from the Mediterranean. In Asia it extends east into the Caucasus and the Crimea, and occurs in North Africa from Morocco to Tunisia. As this wide distribution indicates, it is a tree of hot dry summers and cool wet winters. In Britain it cannot be relied upon to endure frost, probably because our summers are not hot and dry enough to ripen the wood. Elsewhere in Europe it is grown as a shade tree. The edible fruit is a 'drupe', like cherry. This means that it has a fleshy covering over a hard, bony nut. An oil can be extracted from the seeds. The timber is greyish white, hard and elastic, used for implements such as in cart wheels; it can be turned on a lathe. The long drawn-out tip of the leaves is known as a drip-tip. This feature is usually associated with tropical trees, where it serves to drain water off the leaves during heavy tropical storms. It is rare in temperate trees. In fact, most of the species of *Celtis* do come from tropical or warm temperate regions.

176

The domed crown of a mature nettle tree provides useful shade in areas with hot summers. It has a poor autumn colour.

BARK
Smooth and grey, wrinkled in old trees and may be ridged at the base.

Black mulberry

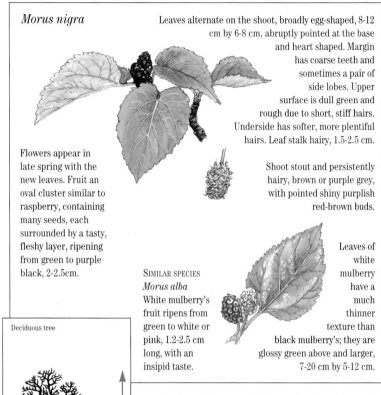

Morus nigra

Leaves alternate on the shoot, broadly egg-shaped, 8-12 cm by 6-8 cm, abruptly pointed at the base and heart shaped. Margin has coarse teeth and sometimes a pair of side lobes. Upper surface is dull green and rough due to short, stiff hairs. Underside has softer, more plentiful hairs. Leaf stalk hairy, 1.5-2.5 cm.

Flowers appear in late spring with the new leaves. Fruit an oval cluster similar to raspberry, containing many seeds, each surrounded by a tasty, fleshy layer, ripening from green to purple black, 2-2.5cm.

Shoot stout and persistently hairy, brown or purple grey, with pointed shiny purplish red-brown buds.

SIMILAR SPECIES
Morus alba
White mulberry's fruit ripens from green to white or pink, 1.2-2.5 cm long, with an insipid taste.

Leaves of white mulberry have a much thinner texture than black mulberry's; they are glossy green above and larger, 7-20 cm by 5-12 cm.

Deciduous tree

8-15 m

Black mulberry could be native to China or to Central Asia, but it was introduced to Europe so long ago that no one really knows its original distribution. It is planted for its fruit, which ripens from late July into September. There are few better tree delights than a mulberry loaded with fruit. Avoid the green and purple-red ones: the ripe ones are black, juicy and stain fingers purple.

   White mulberry is native to China, but, like black mulberry, has been cultivated for centuries. The fruit, though sweet, is insipid. It is best left for the birds. White mulberry's main significance to man is as the preferred food of the silkworm caterpillar. In the East, white mulberries are pruned annually and the leaves stripped from the young shoots to be fed to the silkworms. When mature, these spin themselves a cocoon, from which silky strands are unwound for silk thread. In the 17th century King James of England tried to establish silk manufacture in England. Sadly, he chose black mulberry, which is loathed by the silkworm. Several places in England claim to have black mulberries dating from then: impossible, because the tree lives less than a hundred years.

Black mulberry makes a small tree, usually wider than tall. The trunk normally leans. It quickly looks old and venerable.

BARK
Orange brown, developing orange fissures and scaly or stringy ridges, often with burrs.

Gean or wild cherry

Prunus avium

Fruit (2 cm) ripens in mid summer. It is round, with a juicy covering over the hard, bony seed, ripening to blackish red or yellow-red.

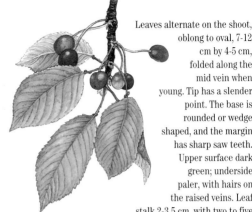

Leaves alternate on the shoot, oblong to oval, 7-12 cm by 4-5 cm, folded along the mid vein when young. Tip has a slender point. The base is rounded or wedge shaped, and the margin has sharp saw teeth. Upper surface dark green; underside paler, with hairs on the raised veins. Leaf stalk 2-3.5 cm, with two to five stalked glands.

Shoot is shiny purple brown, with bluntly pointed egg-shaped buds, 0.5 cm long.

White flowers in mid spring in small clusters with the new foliage, hanging down, 2.5-3.5 cm.

Deciduous tree

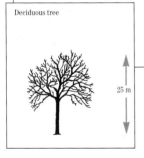

25 m

Native throughout Europe (except for the far north), gean also extends across Russia into Siberia, and it has a natural range in Turkey, northern Iran and North Africa. The fruit can be either sweet or bitter, but is not acid. This is the parent tree for the sweet cherry varieties used in orchards worldwide. It has several common names, including gean, wild cherry and mazzard. The scientific name translates as bird cherry – confusing, since the common name of *Prunus padus,* page 182, is bird cherry.

The tree grows on a range of soils, but on dry, sandy ones it tends to be short lived. The largest trees develop on moisture-retentive clays or loams and can be nearly as big as oak in mixed woodland. The hard, light red timber is excellent, and used for furniture, flooring and sculpture; it fetches more than oak. The seed has a hard case and requires two treatments to germinate. First, a moist, warm period to break down the case; then a cool one to remove the chemicals which inhibit germination. As the seeds ripen in the summer, they can get the first, but often need a second summer to complete the second.

Gean makes a very attractive sight in spring when in full flower and can brighten mixed woodland, orchards or gardens. Branches of young trees are in spaced whorls; on older trees, the crown is rounded, dense and twiggy.

BARK

Shiny, purplish red and peeling slightly in young trees. There are prominent breathing pores (lenticels). Older trees develop grey or black fissures.

Bird cherry

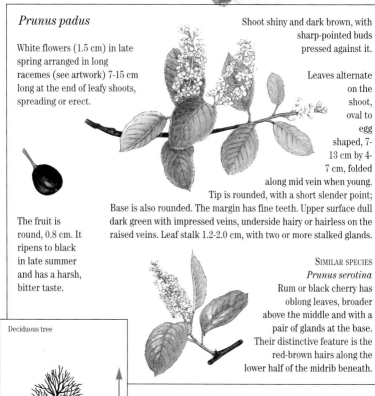

Prunus padus

White flowers (1.5 cm) in late spring arranged in long racemes (see artwork) 7-15 cm long at the end of leafy shoots, spreading or erect.

Shoot shiny and dark brown, with sharp-pointed buds pressed against it.

Leaves alternate on the shoot, oval to egg shaped, 7-13 cm by 4-7 cm, folded along mid vein when young. Tip is rounded, with a short slender point; Base is also rounded. The margin has fine teeth. Upper surface dull dark green with impressed veins, underside hairy or hairless on the raised veins. Leaf stalk 1.2-2.0 cm, with two or more stalked glands.

The fruit is round, 0.8 cm. It ripens to black in late summer and has a harsh, bitter taste.

SIMILAR SPECIES
Prunus serotina
Rum or black cherry has oblong leaves, broader above the middle and with a pair of glands at the base. Their distinctive feature is the red-brown hairs along the lower half of the midrib beneath.

Deciduous tree

10-20 m

This cherry is native throughout Europe except for the Balkans, and extends almost to the far north of Norway and Sweden. It is also native across Siberia into north-eastern China and into the northern Japanese island of Hokkaido. Unsuited to hot or dry sites, it prefers cool, moist places. This is shown by its distribution in Britain, where it only occurs as a common wild tree in the north and west, and is absent, except as planted trees, from the south and east.

Bird cherry contains cyanide in the leaves, fruits and wood – to some extent a feature of all *Prunus* species. Only in a few species, for example bitter almonds, is the quantity enough to be dangerous.

Rum or black cherry is native to the eastern half of North America from Nova Scotia south to Florida and west to Arizona and Dakota; it is naturalized in several parts of Britain and Europe. It makes a much larger tree than bird cherry, but has similar flowers and fruits. It is easily separated. The scientific name, *serotina*, means late, and refers to its habit of leafing late in spring. The common name arises from the fruit's former use as a flavouring for rum.

Bird cherry is planted as an ornamental tree for its showy white flowers. They can almost obliterate the leaves. It is frequently wider than tall when planted as an ornamental.

BARK
Dark grey-brown and smooth, becoming fissured If cut, it smells acrid.

Japanese cherry

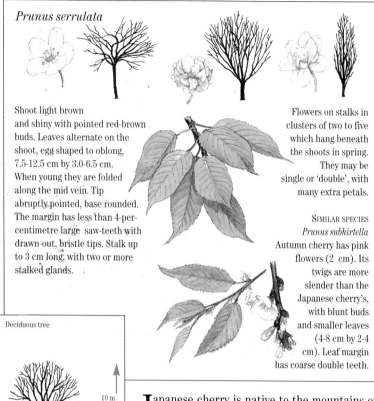

Prunus serrulata

Shoot light brown and shiny with pointed red-brown buds. Leaves alternate on the shoot, egg-shaped to oblong, 7.5-12.5 cm by 3.0-6.5 cm. When young they are folded along the mid vein. Tip abruptly pointed, base rounded. The margin has less than 4-per-centimetre large saw-teeth with drawn-out, bristle tips. Stalk up to 3 cm long, with two or more stalked glands.

Flowers on stalks in clusters of two to five which hang beneath the shoots in spring. They may be single or 'double', with many extra petals.

SIMILAR SPECIES
Prunus subhirtella
Autumn cherry has pink flowers (2 cm). Its twigs are more slender than the Japanese cherry's, with blunt buds and smaller leaves (4-8 cm by 2-4 cm). Leaf margin has coarse double teeth.

Deciduous tree

10 m

Japanese cherry is native to the mountains of Japan, also to central and northern China and Korea. In these isolated areas the trees vary and are usually assigned to different varieties. The wild tree tends to have excellent autumn colour, but the garden forms are less reliable, selected firstly for their gaudy flowers.

A selection of the garden forms, or *sato zakura* (Japanese for garden cherries), would include: 'Amanogawa', with erect branches making a narrow upright tree up to 8 m with pale pink flowers; 'Kanzan', with purplish-pink flowers on a semi-erect vase-shaped crown – this has been too widely planted; 'Shirofugen', with arching, hanging branches and deep rose-pink double flowers which fade to dull whitish pink; 'Shirotae', with a spreading crown and intense white hanging flowers; 'Taihaku' with large, white single flowers, largest in the group; and 'Ukon', with curious greenish- yellow flowers.

Prunus subhirtella is mainly grown as the autumn cherry, 'Autumnalis', giving a succession of flowers in mild periods from late autumn. 'Rosea' normally flowers in spring.

Japanese cherries occur in a large range of flower and habit forms. The crown varies from the narrow upright of 'Amanogawa' to the spreading 'Ukon' and 'Tai-Haku'. In 'Kanzan' the crown is a semi-erect vase shaped, but droops on old trees.

BARK
Brown, with prominent horizontal lenticels or breathing pores, smooth in young trees but rougher in old trees.

Pear

Pyrus communis

Fruit pear shaped or rounded with an indented base. Green and russet coloured, with many breathing pores (lenticels) Remains of flowers persist at the tip.

Shoot glossy brown, later grey brown, with shiny, pointed red-brown buds. Leaves alternate on the shoot, a rounded egg-shape to oval, 4-8 cm by 4-5 cm; tip rounded or with a short point. Base is rounded or a shallow heart-shape. Margin is either untoothed or with very fine teeth. Leaf stalk (1.5-4 cm), oval in section and yellow green in colour.

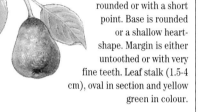

White flowers appear in small clusters before the leaves.

SIMILAR SPECIES
Pyrus cordata
Plymouth pear has egg-shaped leaves only 2.5-5.5 cm by 1.5-3.5 cm with rounded teeth. Much smaller (rounded) fruits (0.8-1.8 cm) than pear, with a hollowd at the tip where the flower parts have fallen. Spiky spur shoots.

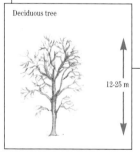

Deciduous tree

12-25 m

The pear is widely cultivated over Europe and into western Asia. Whether this represents its native distribution is less clear, and it is possible that the orchard pear, as described here, is actually a complex hybrid involving several pear species from Southern and Eastern Europe and western Asia. The orchard varieties comprise several hundred different forms, all varying in their fruit size, texture, ripening and taste. However, they share the leathery, glossy leaves; the only other tree commonly encountered with rather similar leaves is the Italian alder (page 110); but they are easy to tell apart because of the alder's catkins and woody, cone-like fruit. Pears have thick-walled cells (grit cells) in the fruits, which are not found in orchard apples. The fruit tends to ripen rather quickly and is very juicy - best eaten over the kitchen sink. The fruits can be fermented to make perry and this is distilled to make calvados.

Plymouth pear is a small tree, mainly found from western France south into Spain and Portugal. There are a few trees in old hedgerows near Plymouth in Devon and Truro in Cornwall, and it may be native there.

Pear is most attractive in early spring when flowering before the leaves expand. It makes an upright, small to medium tree, spiky when young, but dense and leafy with a rounded crown when old.

BARK
Brown or black, quickly becoming cracked into small square plates or scales.

Whitebeam

Sorbus aria

Leaves alternate along the shoot and cluster near the tip. They are oval to egg-shaped, 6-12 cm by 3-8 cm, bluntly pointed at the tip and wedge-shaped or rounded at the base. The margin is sharply saw-toothed with larger teeth at the ends of the eight to 13 pairs of veins. The upper surface soon loses its white hairs, but these remain on the underside. Leaf stalk is 1-2 cm long.

Many small, dull white flowers in heads 5-10 cm across, May/June. Fruit egg-shaped, 0.8-1.5 cm, ripening to scarlet-red.

Shoot covered by dense white hairs when new, but they are soon lost to be replaced by brown, rounded-pointed buds. These are green and brown, with some white hairs.

SIMILAR SPECIES
Sorbus intermedia

Swedish whitebeam leaves are oval, 7-12 cm by 5-7 cm. The margin has five to seven large, rounded teeth, which reach a quarter of the distance to the midrib. The underside is a dense grey white, and woolly.

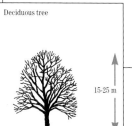

Deciduous tree

15-25 m

Whitebeam is native to southern England and to County Galway in Ireland, and on the mainland of Europe from southern Germany east to Romania and into the Balkans; also south through France into Spain. It also occurs in Morocco and Algeria. It will grow happily on acid sands and other sites, but is most frequent on chalk or limestone. The tree's distinctive feature is its dense white 'wool'. This is most striking in the new foliage (especially in the form 'Lutescens', common as a street tree). The wool soon falls from most parts, but persists under the leaves. The tree's common name refers to the wool: 'beam' is the old Anglo-Saxon word for tree (the German word *Baum* and the Dutch word *boom* have the same origin).

Swedish whitebeam is native to southern Sweden and from Denmark to Poland on the southern side of the Baltic. It is a hybrid, probably between whitebeam and rowan, and has an odd breeding pattern: the seeds only inherit genetic material from their mother. An extremely tough tree, it tolerates poor sites and gives an attractive display of flowers and red berries.

Whitebeam is mainly seen as an ornamental in streets and parks, where its low, rounded crown is typical. It is also a woodland tree, especially on chalk and limestone, and is the only tree commonly found growing with yew on chalk downland (page 49).

BARK
Smooth and grey; on old trees becoming scaly, with fissures at the base.

Crab apple

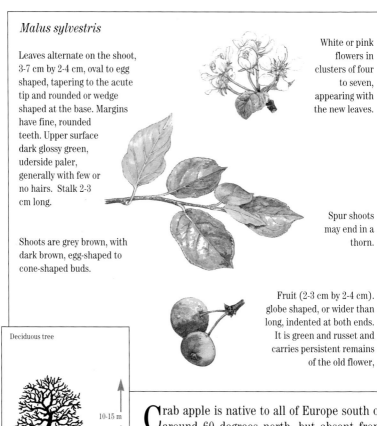

Malus sylvestris

Leaves alternate on the shoot, 3-7 cm by 2-4 cm, oval to egg shaped, tapering to the acute tip and rounded or wedge shaped at the base. Margins have fine, rounded teeth. Upper surface dark glossy green, uderside paler, generally with few or no hairs. Stalk 2-3 cm long.

Shoots are grey brown, with dark brown, egg-shaped to cone-shaped buds.

White or pink flowers in clusters of four to seven, appearing with the new leaves.

Spur shoots may end in a thorn.

Fruit (2-3 cm by 2-4 cm). globe shaped, or wider than long, indented at both ends. It is green and russet and carries persistent remains of the old flower,

Deciduous tree

10-15 m

Crab apple is native to all of Europe south of around 60 degrees north, but absent from Portugal and adjacent regions of Spain. Further east it occurs along the Black Sea coast of Turkey and Georgia, and along the southern shore of the Caspian in northern Iran. It is one of the parent species of the domestic apple, sharing with it the indented base where the fruit is attached to the stalk. However, the orchard apple is much hairier in all its parts, and generally makes a much smaller tree. Crab apple has rather small fruits, but as it hybridizes with the orchard apple, you may come across crab apples with larger fruits. . The fruit has a rubbery texture and a sour taste; it is not eaten fresh, but can be used to make cider and jellies.

The tree grows in mixed broadleaved woodland and in Britain is often on ancient woodland sites – woods for which there is documentary evidence that they existed before 1600 AD. The timber is not available in large sizes. Heavy and difficult to work, it is a pinkish-red colour. Crab apple is rarely planted, although ornamental crabs are widely used in streets and parks.

Crab apple develops a domed, leafy crown, rounded in old trees but more conical and spiky in young ones. *Malus domestica*, the orchard apple, has much bigger fruit and is hairy in all its parts.

BARK
Smooth and green brown with large orange breathing pores (lenticels) in young trees, becoming brown and cracked in old trees.

Silver lime

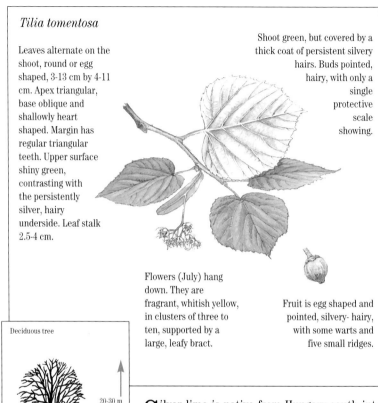

Tilia tomentosa

Leaves alternate on the shoot, round or egg shaped, 3-13 cm by 4-11 cm. Apex triangular, base oblique and shallowly heart shaped. Margin has regular triangular teeth. Upper surface shiny green, contrasting with the persistently silver, hairy underside. Leaf stalk 2.5-4 cm.

Shoot green, but covered by a thick coat of persistent silvery hairs. Buds pointed, hairy, with only a single protective scale showing.

Flowers (July) hang down. They are fragrant, whitish yellow, in clusters of three to ten, supported by a large, leafy bract.

Fruit is egg shaped and pointed, silvery- hairy, with some warts and five small ridges.

Deciduous tree

20-30 m

Silver lime is native from Hungary south into the Balkans and north-western Turkey – and north into south-western Russia. It is the only European silver lime. Silver limes get their common name from the silvery hairs which initially cover all parts of the tree, but are only reliably persistent on the underside of the leaves. Look at them under a handlens. (This is easiest if you choose a piece, such as a shoot, which does not have dense hairs.) Notice that they have several 'arms' which radiate out from the middle like the rays of a star. The scientific name, *tomentosa,* means hairy.

Silver lime is planted as an ornamental tree and makes a dense crown, with strongly fragrant flowers. Unfortunately, and especially in dry summers, the nectar contains a sugar which the common bumblebee is unable to digest. Its accumulation intoxicates and may kill the bees. Lime wood is white and soft, easily moulded and makes the best wood carvings, such as those by Grinling Gibbons, the celebrated 17th-century wood carver. A form of chocolate has been produced from the seeds, but was unsuccessful as it did not keep.

Silver lime makes a large ornamental tree which is very effective in a slight breeze when the silver undersides of the leaves are displayed. The cultivar 'Petiolaris' (shown here) has branches which hang down at the ends and also long leaf stalks, which allow the leaves to hang.

BARK
Grey green and smooth, but with some lines (striations). In older trees it becomes grey, with a network of flat ridges.

Small-leaved lime

Tilia cordata

Leaves alternate on the shoot, a rounded egg shape to a triangular egg shape, 3-8 cm by 3-8 cm. Apex has an abrupt, slender point, base is oblique and deeply heart shaped Margin has regular, sharp teeth. Upper surface matt and somewhat bluish green, underside bluish with red or orange tufts (axils) in the junction of the veins. Leaf stalk 2-4 cm.

Flowers fragrant and whitish cream in July. Held level, with or above the leaves, in clusters of five to 11 with a large, leafy bract.

Fruit oval to round, smooth, with a thin shell. No ridges.

Shoot green and soon without hairs. Buds bluntly pointed, green with only two protective scales showing.

SIMILAR SPECIES
Tilia platyphyllos
Leaves of large-leaved lime are a broad egg shape and larger than small-leaved lime's, 6-15 cm by 7-13 cm. They have a dense covering of simple hairs on both surfaces.

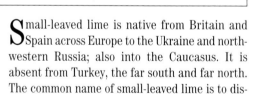

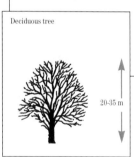

Deciduous tree

20-35 m

Small-leaved lime is native from Britain and Spain across Europe to the Ukraine and north-western Russia; also into the Caucasus. It is absent from Turkey, the far south and far north.

The common name of small-leaved lime is to distinguish it from the large-leaved lime, which has a similar distribution except that it is found in Turkey. Both species have been managed in woodlands as coppiced trees – they are cut down to ground level every few years and allowed to sprout. The stumps can be 6 m across and perhaps 2,000 years old, although in such large stumps the centre rots away leaving an incomplete ring of stems. Coppicing was carried out partly for the wood, but more especially for the bark. This was stripped off the stems and rotted, leaving the fibres, which were twisted into rope.

Small- and large-leaved limes have produced a hybrid, *T. europaea*. This is known as common lime, since it is common in cultivation (although rare in the wild). Its leaves are shiny with axillary brown tufts on the underside, and less hairy. The tree produces an excess of basal suckers and honeydew.

Small-leaved lime occurs naturally in woodland, but is most often seen as a specimen tree. It can be used for avenues. The crown is rounded, usually taller than broad, unlike the tree shown here.

BARK
Grey and smooth on young trees, becoming darker and fissuring into scaly plates on old trees.

Phillyrea

Phillyrea latifolia

Leaves are in opposite pairs, egg shaped through to lance shaped in outline, 1.5-6 cm by 1-4 cm. Margin may be untoothed, or with sharp or rounded teeth. Upper surface mid to deep shiny green, underside paler, with glandular dots. Stalk 0.5-0.6 cm.

Shoot grey brown and finely hairy when young, later dark grey, flattened beside the small, pointed buds.

Flowers in late winter or early spring in short clusters in the axils of last year's leaves. They are white or yellow, and very small (0.2 cm).

Fruit is a drupe (a hard nut with a fleshy coat), ripening to blue black in first autumn, 0.6-1.0 cm.

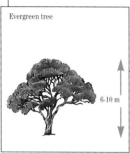

Evergreen tree

6-10 m

hillyrea is native to the Mediterranean region from Portugal in the west to western Asia in the east, also to North Africa. It is characteristic of the *maquis*, which, strictly speaking, is an association of evergreen shrubs on dry, rocky hillsides, and which characterizes much of the Mediterranean landscape. *Maquis* shrubs are noted for their hard, glossy leaves, an adaptation to restrict water loss. Frequently, phillyrea is no more than a low shrub, but on better sites it can make a small tree. The name derives from Classical legend: Philyra, a beautiful sea nymph, bore a son to the god Kronos. It was half man, half horse. Appalled by its appearance, she prayed to be turned into a tree – and was.

The timber is rarely available in any size or quantity, and, when it is, the unpleasant smell discourages use. It is one of the few timbers which weighs more than water. Phillyrea is closely related to the privets (*Ligustrum*), a mainly shrubby genus commonest as a garden plant. The easiest way to separate them is by the flowers: those of *Ligustrum* are terminal on the shoots (or side shoots); those of phillyrea are carried in the leaf axils – see above.

On cultivation, phillyrea makes a
neat, small tree with a rounded
crown. It is valued as an
evergreen, but not for floral
beauty.

BARK
Smooth and dark grey,
becoming finely fissured
and cracking into small
squares.

Olive

Olea europaea

Leaves are in opposite pairs,
lance shaped to a narrow egg
shape in outline, 2-8 cm by
0.8-2 cm. Margin untoothed,
upper surface grey green,
underside white with dense
scales. Leaf stalk short.

Fragrant flowers
appear in clusters
in the axils of the
current year's growths.

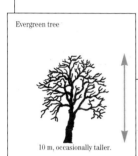

Shoot silvery grey, with a
dense covering of scales,
becoming brown when these
have rubbed off. It is round or
four-angled in section, with
small buds.

Fruit is a drupe (a hard nut with a
fleshy coat), egg shaped to round,
(1.0-3.5 cm), ripening over 12
months or longer from green to
black or brown; oily flesh.

Evergreen tree

10 m, occasionally taller.

This tree is so characteristic of the Mediterranean landscape that it would be natural to
assume that it is a native of the region. In fact, it
is more likely to have been introduced at an early
stage from the Arabian peninsula, where it seems
to be native in the dry, barren mountains between Saudi Arabia and Yemen.
Wild olives are found here in apparently natural settings: they have smaller
leaves than planted ones, and spiny shoots. The tree cannot tolerate more than
a few degrees of frost, and like other plants which thrive in hot places, it does
not put up with shade. It is very tolerant of drought once established, ideally
suited to the wet winters/dry hot summers of the Mediterranean climate.

As is well known, the tree is important worldwide as the source of olive oil,
which is pressed from the fleshy covering of the fruit, and considered the best
of the vegetable oils, containing many polyunsaturates. These are said to be
better for the body than other types of fat, but nonetheless still seem to add
to one's girth. The wood is black or brown. It polishes well and is used for small
items or joinery, or for flooring and panelling.

Olives trees are often pollarded when raised in groves. This simplifies fruit collection – and makes for small, dense crowns on stout boles.

BARK
Silvery grey, becoming finely fissured and fluted, with crossing ridges that give deep, dark hollows.

Strawberry tree

Arbutus unedo
Leaves set alternately on the green or pink shoots, oval to egg shaped in outline, 5-10 cm by 1.5-4 cm. They are rounded at the tip and wedge-shaped at the base, with forward-pointing, sharp teeth. Upper surface leathery and dark green, underside light green. Leaf stalk (0.7-1 cm) is pink.

Fruit round and rough like a strawberry, 1.5-2.0 cm, ripening in the second autumn at the same time as flowering.

White or pink bell-shaped flowers from October to December in small clusters of 15-20.

SIMILAR SPECIES
Arbutus andrachne
Leaves of Greek or Cyprus strawberry tree stiff (not leathery) and wider than strawberry tree's.

Leaves of Greek strawberry tree are waxy blue- white underneath, with 'net' veining. Margin untoothed or only finely toothed, 4-10 cm by 2-6 cm. Leaf stalk 2-4 cm, grooved.

Evergreen tree

8-13 m

This species is native around the shores of the Mediterranean region from Portugal to Turkey and Cyprus; also in North Africa. It is also found in south-western Ireland around Killarney in County Kerry and is believed to have sat out the last ice age on islands off the Irish coast. It is happily naturalized on the barren sandy soils found in England around Poole and Bournemouth.

Strawberry tree is a dull evergreen for most of the year, but achieves a rare double in the autumn when the new flowers are carried at the time of peak ripening of last summer's fruit. The fruits can be used to make preserves. They are edible, but Linnaeus, the great Swedish botanist, had it just about right when he coined the specific name *unedo*, which means I eat one.

Cyprus or Greek strawberry tree is native to the eastern Mediterranean. Apart from the foliage differences shown above, the flowers are carried in larger clusters and open in the spring from buds laid down in the previous year. The fruits ripen in autumn, giving the tree two seasons of floral display. The bark is also much superior, being red and smooth.

Strawberry tree makes an
evergreen tree which tolerates
hot, dry sites. It has a low, rounded
crown, often broader than tall.

BARK
Dark red, shredding as the
tree matures. May be scaly
with grey brown ridges on
old trees.

Judas tree

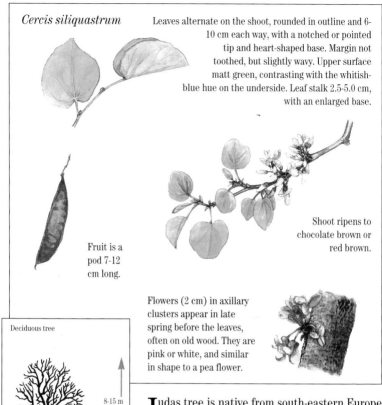

Cercis siliquastrum

Leaves alternate on the shoot, rounded in outline and 6-10 cm each way, with a notched or pointed tip and heart-shaped base. Margin not toothed, but slightly wavy. Upper surface matt green, contrasting with the whitish-blue hue on the underside. Leaf stalk 2.5-5.0 cm, with an enlarged base.

Shoot ripens to chocolate brown or red brown.

Fruit is a pod 7-12 cm long.

Flowers (2 cm) in axillary clusters appear in late spring before the leaves, often on old wood. They are pink or white, and similar in shape to a pea flower.

Deciduous tree

8-15 m

Judas tree is native from south-eastern Europe to western Asia, where it is found in a band running close to the Mediterranean coast from the eastern shore of the Adriatic through to southern Israel. It also occurs on both sides of the Bosphorus and on the Crimea in the northern Black Sea. It favours hot, dry sites and does not like prolonged periods of severe frost. Legend has it that this is tree on which Judas Iscariot hanged himself, hence the common name. The name may also allude to the way in which the flowers and fruits hang down. Another possibility is that the name refers to Judaea in the southern part both of Israel and the tree's natural range. The genus name, *Cercis,* is from the Greek word for a weaver's shuttle and refers to the shape of the fruit.

The timber is hard and tough, red overall, but with beautifully dark veins: prized in joinery. The tree is planted as an ornamental and is unusual in that it flowers from the older wood. Often, flowers are produced straight from the trunk, whereas nearly all other temperate trees only produce flowers on the current or previous year's growths.

Judas tree makes a fine display in late spring when the twigs and often the main branches are wreathed with the flowers. The trunk often leans, putting the rounded crown off centre.

BARK
Grey brown, smooth, cracking into small brown squares.

Orange

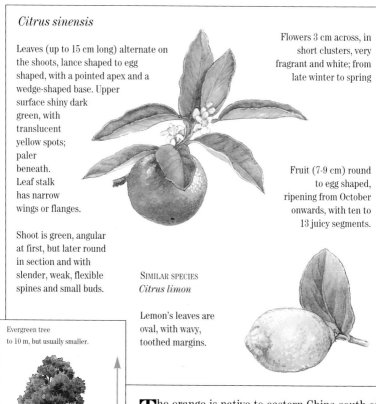

Citrus sinensis

Leaves (up to 15 cm long) alternate on the shoots, lance shaped to egg shaped, with a pointed apex and a wedge-shaped base. Upper surface shiny dark green, with translucent yellow spots; paler beneath. Leaf stalk has narrow wings or flanges.

Shoot is green, angular at first, but later round in section and with slender, weak, flexible spines and small buds.

Flowers 3 cm across, in short clusters, very fragrant and white; from late winter to spring

Fruit (7-9 cm) round to egg shaped, ripening from October onwards, with ten to 13 juicy segments.

SIMILAR SPECIES
Citrus limon

Lemon's leaves are oval, with wavy, toothed margins.

Evergreen tree to 10 m, but usually smaller.

The orange is native to eastern China south of the River Yangtze or 'Golden Sands river', but of course has been widely cultivated in Europe for a very long time. It was probably introduced to Europe before Roman times. The fruit, known as a 'hesperid', is unique to the genus *Citrus*. It consists of eight to 15 segments surrounded by a whitish pith and a zest or outer skin which contains many gland cells. The seeds are carried in the segments. The juicy bits of the segments are believed to derive from enlarged hair cells. The leaves are also unusual in being jointed between the leaf stalk and the blade; and the stalk often has wings or flanges which function as part of the leaf area. Indeed in some species of orange the winged stalk has nearly the same area as the leaf blade; in fact, the grapefruit is one of these.

The lemon has a similar long history of cultivation to the orange, and is believed to have come from south-eastern China. The acid flesh and the characteristic shape are sure means of identification. When in flower, lemon can be separated by its 25-40 stamens, compared to only 20 in the orange.

Oranges cultivated in groves are rarely allowed to grow more than a few metres in height because this simplifies harvesting. The bushes may carry fruits and flowers at the same time.

BARK
Grey, smooth or wrinkled.

Cider gum

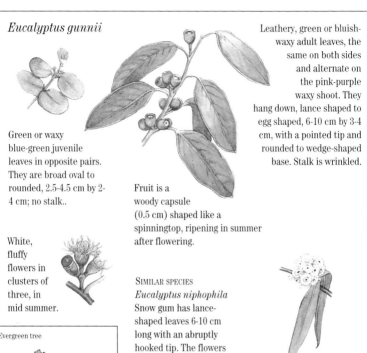

Eucalyptus gunnii

Green or waxy blue-green juvenile leaves in opposite pairs. They are broad oval to rounded, 2.5-4.5 cm by 2-4 cm; no stalk..

Leathery, green or bluish-waxy adult leaves, the same on both sides and alternate on the pink-purple waxy shoot. They hang down, lance shaped to egg shaped, 6-10 cm by 3-4 cm, with a pointed tip and rounded to wedge-shaped base. Stalk is wrinkled.

Fruit is a woody capsule (0.5 cm) shaped like a spinningtop, ripening in summer after flowering.

White, fluffy flowers in clusters of three, in mid summer.

SIMILAR SPECIES
Eucalyptus niphophila
Snow gum has lance-shaped leaves 6-10 cm long with an abruptly hooked tip. The flowers and fruits are in clusters of seven or more.

Evergreen tree

20-30 m

Cider gum is native to Tasmania and south-eastern mainland Australia. It is one of the hardiest of the many species of eucalypts and is the commonest eucalyptus species in Britain. The name eucalyptus literally means 'fused petals'. These are not showy and large as in most flowers. Instead, they form a cap over the developing flower bud which, in due course, falls off as the flower opens. The other unusual feature of eucalypts is the foliage. Most trees have two types of leaves: seed leaves (the first pair of leaves produced as the seed germinates), and adult leaves. Eucalypts manage seed, juvenile and adult leaves, and intermediates. Juvenile leaves (see above) give way to the adult leaves, which have stalks and are similar on both sides. When a eucalypt is cut back, the first leaves it makes are juvenile ones, however old the tree. The strongly clustered and coloured juvenile leaves are favoured by flower arrangers.

Snow gum is native to south-eastern mainland Australia. It is generally a small tree, making only 10 m. Its main attraction is the snow-white colour of the newly-exposed bark.

Thre tree's new shoots have only a few small leaves, giving a halo effect over the denser crown of a fast-growing tree. Young trees are very narrow and upright, but they become rounded as they mature.

BARK
At first pale green or cream coloured beneath, but gradually changing to grey before being shed in large sheets.

Tasmanian blue gum

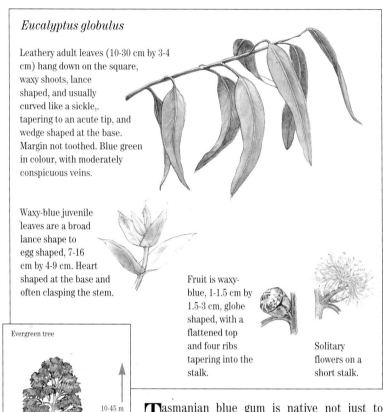

Eucalyptus globulus

Leathery adult leaves (10-30 cm by 3-4 cm) hang down on the square, waxy shoots, lance shaped, and usually curved like a sickle,. tapering to an acute tip, and wedge shaped at the base. Margin not toothed. Blue green in colour, with moderately conspicuous veins.

Waxy-blue juvenile leaves are a broad lance shape to egg shaped, 7-16 cm by 4-9 cm. Heart shaped at the base and often clasping the stem.

Fruit is waxy-blue, 1-1.5 cm by 1.5-3 cm, globe shaped, with a flattened top and four ribs tapering into the stalk.

Solitary flowers on a short stalk.

Evergreen tree

10-45 m

Tasmanian blue gum is native not just to Tasmania, but also to a single area in Victoria on the mainland of south-eastern Australia. It is probably the most widely cultivated of the eucalypts, growing well in climates which are not cold in winter. In Britain it rarely survives for more than three or four years, except in the mildest parts, before being killed by winter cold. However, it can grow to 10 m in this time, presenting a large corpse for removal. In Britain it may benefit from global warming. In north-eastern Spain and other warm areas it is commonly grown as a timber tree, especially for pulp. The trees are harvested every few years and coppicing results in vigorous regrowth from the stump without the need for replanting. Although in Britain and northern Europe the tree is not hardy, it is widely planted in summer bedding schemes for its blue foliage, growing to 2 or 3 metres by the autumn. It is unique amongst the six hundred or so eucalypts in having single flowers and fruits. All the other species have between three and 15 flowers in a cluster. The fruits are also larger and distinctively ribbed and warty.

As a young tree, Tasmanian blue gum has a very narrow crown with a single trunk. In the open (as here) it develops a rounded crown.

BARK
This is shed to show white beneath, which gradually matures through fawn, pink and grey to grey-brown before shedding once more.

Campbell's magnolia

Magnolia campbellii

Oval leaves alternate on the shoot, 15-33 cm by 8-15 cm. Apex acute, base wedge-shaped. Margin untoothed and translucent. Upper surface somewhat shiny green, underside waxy-green, with around 20 raised hairy veins which do not extend to the margin. Leaf stalk 3-6 cm, enlarged at the base.

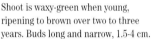

Flowers appear from buds at the end of last season's shoots in late winter, before the leaves. They are 20-30 cm across, with 12-16 pink or white petals, prone to frost damage.

Fruit cylindrical, 15-20 cm.

Shoot is waxy-green when young, ripening to brown over two to three years. Buds long and narrow, 1.5-4 cm.

SIMILAR SPECIES

Magnolia acuminata
Leaves of cucumber tree light green or yellow-green, 8-25 cm by 5-11 cm, with ten to 14 pairs of veins. Erect, yellow-green flowers at the end of leafy shoots in June.

Deciduous tree

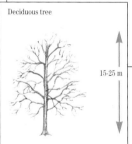

15-25 m

This species is native of the Himalayas from eastern Nepal through Sikkim and Bhutan, with a subspecies extending the range through north-eastern India and Burma into Yunnan, Western China. It occurs in a warm temperate zone with a high summer rainfall, and snow in winter — but not too cold. It is slow to flower when raised from seed, taking around 25 years. The eastern sub-species (*mollicomata*) will flower at half this age, but the blooms have a muddy purple tint. The wood has no special uses, but the Chinese use the bark of this and other *Magnolia* species as herbal medicines.

Magnolia acuminata comes from eastern North America. The flowers are carried after the leaves have emerged and therefore much less visible. The common name, cucumber tree, refers to the appearance of the young fruits.

Saucer magnolia (*Magnolia soulangiana*) and Kobushi (*Magnolia kobus*) are two magnolias which flower on the bare branches. Saucer magnolia is commonest in cultivation; the usual form has disappointing flowers – white with a pink-purple tinge. Kobushi is from Japan and has fine white flowers.

Campbell's magnolia is stunning in late winter when loaded with its large blooms, but such displays can be ruined by frost. The crown is column-shaped, with a cone-shaped tip (as seen here) until in old age it becomes broader and more rounded.

BARK
Light grey or grey brown, smooth or finely wrinkled, only fissured and scaly at the base of old trees.

Bull bay or evergreen magnolia

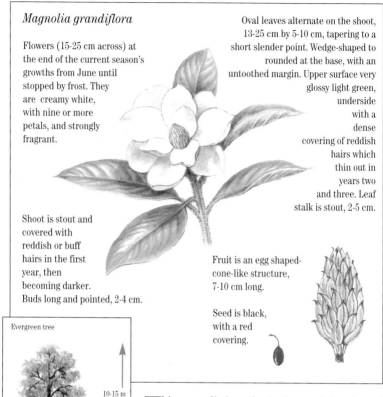

Magnolia grandiflora

Flowers (15-25 cm across) at the end of the current season's growths from June until stopped by frost. They are creamy white, with nine or more petals, and strongly fragrant.

Oval leaves alternate on the shoot, 13-25 cm by 5-10 cm, tapering to a short slender point. Wedge-shaped to rounded at the base, with an untoothed margin. Upper surface very glossy light green, underside with a dense covering of reddish hairs which thin out in years two and three. Leaf stalk is stout, 2-5 cm.

Shoot is stout and covered with reddish or buff hairs in the first year, then becoming darker. Buds long and pointed, 2-4 cm.

Fruit is an egg shaped-cone-like structure, 7-10 cm long.

Seed is black, with a red covering.

Evergreen tree

10-15 m

This magnolia is native to the coastal regions of south-eastern U.S.A. from North Carolina south to Florida along the Atlantic coast and along the Gulf of Mexico coast to Texas. It occurs in moist lowland valley sites where it is associated with other broadleaved tree species and is much hardier than you might expect, given its southern origin. The tree is grown for its combination of glossy leaves and large flowers. It has been cultivated in Britain and Western Europe for centuries and has produced a number of cultivars. These vary in leaf size and shape, and in the density of the reddish or rufous hairs on the leaf underside (an attractive feature). In fact, they are all useful ornamental trees because they produce deliciously scented blooms in succession through the summer. Examples include 'Exmouth', which has narrow leaves and makes a more upright tree; and 'Goliath', with suitably sized (30-cm) blooms. The scientific name refers to the large flowers: when named, it had the largest of any known species. The name bull bay refers to the glossy foliage, vaguely similar to that of bay laurel, but much larger. It is also known as southern magnolia.

Bull bay has an upright crown with the lower branches slightly drooping. It is often grown beside walls, but will also do well as a free-standing tree.

BARK
Light brown, becoming rough and scaly at the base.

Tulip tree

Liriodendron tulipiferum

Flowers (4-5 cm) terminate the current seasons's growths in early summer. They have six green to yellow petals.

Leaves alternate on the shoot, 7-20 cm broad and long. They have a very distinctive shape, indented or cut-off at the tip, wedge shaped to heart shaped at the base and with two pairs of acute lobes. Upper surface shiny green, lower surface bluish green. Leaf stalk 5-10 cm, with an enlarged base.

Deciduous tree

25-30 m

Shoot glossy brown, with oval, flattened bluish-green buds on 1-cm stalks.

Fruit is cone-like, 4-5 cm.

Tulip tree is native to eastern North America from Nova Scotia and southern Ontario south to Florida and Louisiana. Within this range, it occurs on well-drained but moist lowland valley sites, where it can reach upwards of 45 m. The name tulip tree refers to the appearance of the flower. These are quite attractive in detail, but often hidden by the foliage. It is also known in the States as yellow poplar, after its appearance during the autumn, when it goes yellow gold. It is also planted for the pale yellow timber: of moderate quality, it is used for furniture and is resistant to woodworm. Tulip tree is an example of the close relationship between the flora of eastern North America and China. The genus contains only two species. The other, *Liriodendron chinense*, is native from eastern China south into Vietnam. Its leaves generally have a narrower waist between the middle pairs of lobes and are a more waxy-blue beneath.

Tulip tree is planted as an ornamental and can make interesting avenues. However, unless named clones are used, trees raised from seed tend to be too variable to make neat rows.

Young tulip trees have a neat column shape, but as they get older they develop a more rounded habit, without low branches. This means that the flowers are often out of reach of the ground.

BARK
Grey brown or grey; smooth on young trees, becoming grey or silvery-grey, with platy scales at the base and orange-brown fissures.

Holly

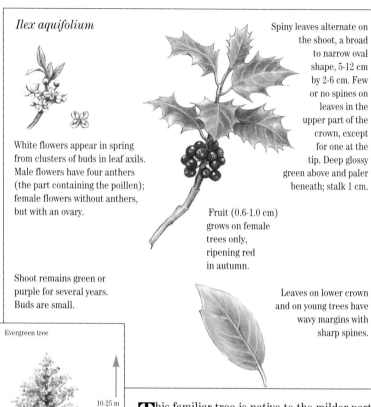

Ilex aquifolium

White flowers appear in spring from clusters of buds in leaf axils. Male flowers have four anthers (the part containing the poillen); female flowers without anthers, but with an ovary.

Shoot remains green or purple for several years. Buds are small.

Spiny leaves alternate on the shoot, a broad to narrow oval shape, 5-12 cm by 2-6 cm. Few or no spines on leaves in the upper part of the crown, except for one at the tip. Deep glossy green above and paler beneath; stalk 1 cm.

Fruit (0.6-1.0 cm) grows on female trees only, ripening red in autumn.

Leaves on lower crown and on young trees have wavy margins with sharp spines.

Evergreen tree

10-25 m

This familiar tree is native to the milder parts of Western Europe from the southern coast of Norway south to Spain and Portugal, and east across southern Europe to the Black Sea. It is also native to North Africa and Turkey on both the Black Sea and Mediterranean coasts. However, it does not occur in Central and Northern Europe, where the winters are too cold for it. People's usual picture of holly is spiny leaves and red berries: true in part. Some trees retain spiny leaves, but in most of them the leaves in the upper crown have very few or no spines. The purpose of the spines is to deter browsing by large mammals, and, as giraffes are not native to Europe, the tree does not need the spines except on the 3 to 4 metres of foliage closest to the ground. Making spines expends the tree's energy, so it doesn't bother with them where they are redundant. The red berries are only found on female trees (and some garden selections have yellow or amber berries). The role of the male trees is to pollinate the flowers. Holly has an easily-worked grey timber which ages to brown. It takes stain well and is used in sculpture and cabinet-making.

Holly makes an upright evergreen tree in woods and hedgerows. Mainly seen as a small tree, it can grow to 25 m or so in sheltered woods. It can easily be trimmed into hedges or topiary.

BARK
Grey and smooth, but with small pimples, becoming silvery grey on old trees.

217

Indian bean tree

Catalpa bignonioides

Fruit is a hanging
pod, 15-40 cm long,
which opens to
release many small,
two-winged seeds.

Flowers (July) make large terminal
clusters, 20-30 cm.Individual
flowers are tubular, white
(4.0-4.5 cm) with a red
strip and purple dots.
Shoot grey-brown
with small buds
in pairs or
threes.

Floppy leaves in
opposite pairs or in
threes on the shoot,
large and egg shaped,
12-25 cm by 10-18 cm. Margin untoothed
and not lobed. Matt green above, paler and hairy
beneath. Stalk is 5-15 cm.

SIMILAR SPECIES
Catalpa speciosa
Northern catalpa's leaves are
more triangular in outline than
Indian bean tree's, and when
crushed they don't give off the
same unpleasant odour. The
flowers are whiter and larger, but
in smaller clusters.

Deciduous tree

10 m, rarely up to 15 m

Indian bean tree is native to south-eastern U.S.A. from Georgia and Florida west to Alabama and Mississippi, where it occurs at the margins of woods. It has been widely planted outside this native range, and despite its southerly origin it is hardy. With most broadleaved trees, the crown diameter of a tree grown in the open is roughly equal to its height, but this is one of the exceptions where the crown is much broader than tall. The fruits hang down from the old flower trusses like strands of spaghetti. The leaves are thin, easily tattered by the wind, and stay green into the autumn until killed by frost. If crushed, they give off an unpleasant odour. The genus name, *Catalpa,* is the Native American word for the tree, while the flowers are similar to the tropical climber *Bignonia*. Its timber is tough and durable, but coarse-grained.

Northern catalpa is a native of central U.S.A. along the Mississippi valley from Arkansas to Indiana. It makes a more tree-like tree, growing to 10 or 20 m, and has a more conventional width than Indian bean tree. With its northern origin, it has a greater tolerance to cold winters.

Indian bean tree is a glorious sight in July when laden with the large clusters of flowers, but is a dead loss in autumn when the leaves fall without turning any colour except black. The large leaves are thin, and cast only a light shade.

BARK
Pink and brown. Smooth in young trees, developing thin, grey scaly flakes on older trees.

219

Paulownia or foxglove tree

Paulownia tomentosa

Flowers open before the leaves in late spring from clusters formed in the autumn. They are bell-shaped, 4-5 cm, violet to blue purple and delicately scented.

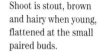

Leaves in opposite pairs, large and egg shaped, 10-35 cm by 10-25 cm, with an acute tip and deeply heart-shaped base. Margin is untoothed, but may have one or two pairs of triangular lobes. Texture thin and floppy, matt green above and paler beneath; hairy. Leaf stalk 10-15 cm.

Shoot is stout, brown and hairy when young, flattened at the small paired buds.

Fruit is a pointed woody capsule (4-5 cm), which opens in the first autumn to release masses of small winged seeds.

Deciduous tree

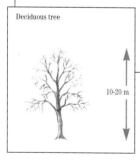

10-20 m

Paulownia is native to northern China, but was an early introduction to Japan and taken from there to Europe in the 1830s. It is a fast-grower. The current season's shoots are pithy. If not cut back before autumn frost arrives, they quickly thicken and produce the fine-grained timber used for delicate implements such as chopsticks. The tree casts only a light shade and is used in agro-forestry as a canopy tree, allowing crops to grow below. In Britain and Europe it is planted as an ornamental. It can also be grown as a shrub, and if cut down in spring it will produce a shoot 2 to 3 m in length, with leaves 60 cm across. The flowers can be damaged by spring frosts, while the leaves fall in autumn at the first hint of cold weather. The genus name is after Princess Anna Paulovna, a daughter of Tsar Paul the First of Russia, whilst the common name refers to the similarity of the flowers to those of the perennial foxglove. It is similar to *Catalpa* (page 218), but the two genera are usually placed in different families. Nonetheless, they are both considered to be close to the ancestral tree from which both families have evolved.

To be fully appreciated, the flowers of this spreading tree need to be seen either against a dark background, or from above. It quickly forms a tall, domed crown.

BARK
Grey or purple, with grey lines; smooth.

London plane

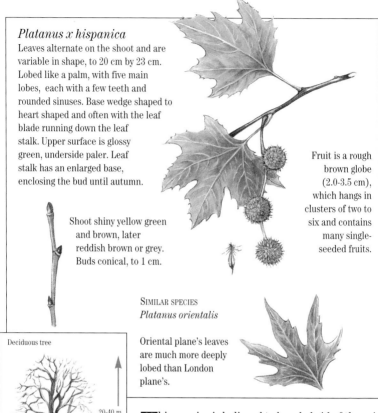

Platanus x hispanica

Leaves alternate on the shoot and are variable in shape, to 20 cm by 23 cm. Lobed like a palm, with five main lobes, each with a few teeth and rounded sinuses. Base wedge shaped to heart shaped and often with the leaf blade running down the leaf stalk. Upper surface is glossy green, underside paler. Leaf stalk has an enlarged base, enclosing the bud until autumn.

Fruit is a rough brown globe (2.0-3.5 cm), which hangs in clusters of two to six and contains many single-seeded fruits.

Shoot shiny yellow green and brown, later reddish brown or grey. Buds conical, to 1 cm.

SIMILAR SPECIES
Platanus orientalis

Oriental plane's leaves are much more deeply lobed than London plane's.

Deciduous tree

20-40 m

This species is believed to be a hybrid of the oriental plane (see below) and the eastern buttonwood from North America, the latter giving it more shallowly-lobed leaves than oriental plane's. It has hybrid vigour and quickly makes a large tree. The seeds are fertile and give rise to seedlings combining the characteristics of the original two species, and a confusing array of forms. It tolerates urban conditions, including atmospheric pollution and excessive pruning, and will grow well on a range of soils. The leaves adopt russet colours in autumn. They are very slow to decompose. The hairs on the new leaves can cause allergic reactions in some people. The timber is of good quality, used for panelling. The tree was for a long time known as *Platanus acerifolia*, from the resemblance of the leaves to certain maples, such as sycamore (*Acer pseudoplatanus*, page 226), and Norway maple (*Acer platanoides*, page 228)).

Oriental plane comes from Greece, Bulgaria, Cyprus and Turkey, and possibly from further east in Asia. It is a tree of valley bottoms, where it grows in moist but well-drained river gravels, which allows it to survive hot summers.

London plane is associated with the squares and parks of London and other major cities, where it makes a large tree capable of complementing the architecture.

BARK
Smooth, shedding in large plates, especially in autumn, to reveal a creamy white which slowly darkens to brown. At the base of old trees, the bark is thicker and scaly, and does not shed.

Sweet gum or liquidambar

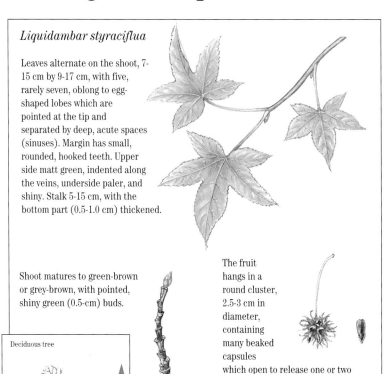

Liquidambar styraciflua

Leaves alternate on the shoot, 7-15 cm by 9-17 cm, with five, rarely seven, oblong to egg-shaped lobes which are pointed at the tip and separated by deep, acute spaces (sinuses). Margin has small, rounded, hooked teeth. Upper side matt green, indented along the veins, underside paler, and shiny. Stalk 5-15 cm, with the bottom part (0.5-1.0 cm) thickened.

Shoot matures to green-brown or grey-brown, with pointed, shiny green (0.5-cm) buds.

The fruit hangs in a round cluster, 2.5-3 cm in diameter, containing many beaked capsules which open to release one or two black winged seeds.

Deciduous tree

20-30 m

This tree is a native of eastern U.S.A., where it occurs from Connecticut across to Illinois and south to Florida and Texas. It is also native to northern and eastern Mexico. The trees from the southern part of its range can be evergreen in mild climates, and generally get their deep autumn colour late. The names (genus, scientific and common) refer to the resin, which can be extracted from the bark. This is used to perfume hides in tanneries and was once used as a chewing gum. The leaves have a resinous scent when crushed. The original source of the resin was the oriental liquidambar, *L. orientalis*, a smaller tree from western and south-western Turkey, and Rhodes. Liquidambar is superficially very similar to several maples, such as sycamore (page 226). However, it can always be separated from the maples by looking at the shoot: on liquidambar, the leaves and buds are arranged alternately along the shoot in a helix, whereas in the maples they are in opposite pairs. It is much closer to plane (page 222), but easily distinguished by the toothed leaf margins and the scaly bark. The base of the leaf stalk does not hide the bud.

Liquidambar is used as a large specimen tree and is particularly attractive in autumn when the dying leaves turn scarlet or red. Young trees (as seen here) are column or cone shaped; old trees have tall, domed crowns.

BARK
Grey, often with weak corky wings when young, becoming rough on old trees, with narrow scaly ridges.

Sycamore

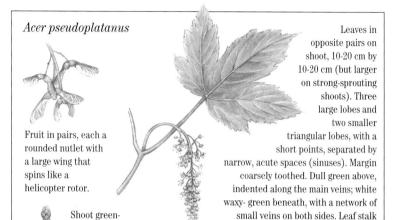

Acer pseudoplatanus

Fruit in pairs, each a rounded nutlet with a large wing that spins like a helicopter rotor.

Shoot green-brown; 0.5-1 cm pointed buds which have green scales with brown tips.

Deciduous tree

15-35 m

Leaves in opposite pairs on shoot, 10-20 cm by 10-20 cm (but larger on strong-sprouting shoots). Three large lobes and two smaller triangular lobes, with a short points, separated by narrow, acute spaces (sinuses). Margin coarsely toothed. Dull green above, indented along the main veins; white waxy- green beneath, with a network of small veins on both sides. Leaf stalk 4-17 cm, with a watery sap.

Flowers in dense, hanging clusters with the new foliage.

SIMILAR SPECIES
Acer opalus
Italian maple's leaves have shallower lobes and fewer teeth than sycamore's. The flowers are a pleasant yellow and appear on the bare branches in early spring.

Sycamore is native from northern Spain in the west to southern Germany; also eastwards across Central and Southern Europe into northern Turkey, and the Caucasus as far as the Caspian Sea. In France it is only native to the central and eastern parts, and in Spain only along the Atlantic coast. It was introduced early to Britain, and naturalized throughout. The winged seeds help to spread the tree far and wide on the wind. A seed produces two large seed leaves (or cotyledons), then normal leaves. As the seeds favour freshly dug soil, they thrive in gardens, to the irritation of gardeners. Sycamore is a very tough tree, tolerating poor, exposed sites, and urban abuse. The foliage is usually covered in tar spots, caused by a fungus, and only occasionally achieves a moderate yellow autumn colour. The high-quality wood is used for panelling and violins.

Italian maple is native to southern and eastern Spain, south-eastern France, southern Switzerland, the Balkans, Italy and North Africa. Its foliage is very similar to sycamore's but easily separated when it flowers in spring: the flowers and fruits are in smaller clusters.

Mature sycamores develop majestic domed crowns, but before this the tree goes through a prolonged stage when the crown is conical and spiky.

BARK
Smooth and silver grey or brown, becoming more and more cracked as the tree ages. Eventually, it has peeling scales, 10-20 cm by 5-10 cm.

Norway maple

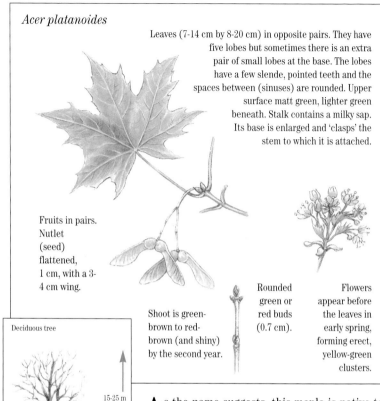

Acer platanoides

Leaves (7-14 cm by 8-20 cm) in opposite pairs. They have five lobes but sometimes there is an extra pair of small lobes at the base. The lobes have a few slende, pointed teeth and the spaces between (sinuses) are rounded. Upper surface matt green, lighter green beneath. Stalk contains a milky sap. Its base is enlarged and 'clasps' the stem to which it is attached.

Fruits in pairs. Nutlet (seed) flattened, 1 cm, with a 3-4 cm wing.

Deciduous tree

15-25 m

Shoot is green-brown to red-brown (and shiny) by the second year.

Rounded green or red buds (0.7 cm).

Flowers appear before the leaves in early spring, forming erect, yellow-green clusters.

As the name suggests, this maple is native to Norway – actually to the south-east of the country. However, its range extends to southern Sweden and east into Russia; also south to the Balkans, central Italy and northern Spain. In France it is native in the east; it is not native to Britain. Widely planted , it naturalizes easily, though is less invasive than sycamore, (page 226). The leaves are similar to sycamore's and London plane's (page 222) but can be separated by the milky sap in the leaf stalk: snap a fresh leaf in half. Actually, it is more closely related to field maple (page 232) and Cappadocian maple (page 230) than to sycamore or plane. Norway maple has given rise to a number of cultivars, especially ones with purple foliage. The best of these (because the purple is transient, replaced by more natural green foliage) is 'Shwedleri', but more common are forms such as 'Crimson King' and 'Goldsworth's Purple', in which the bright purple of spring becomes dull and dank in summer before being lightened by the autumn colour. All the purple forms also have purple bracts with the yellow flowers and are respectable at that stage.

Norway maple makes a domed tree which is particularly attractive when carrying the flowers in early spring. Seen here is a young tree in autumn colour with a typical spiky crown. The tree is planted as an ornamental and is tolerant of poor urban conditions.

BARK
Grey or pinkish-brown grey, smooth on young trees, then becoming folded. Old trees develop shallow fissures and ridges.

Cappadocian maple

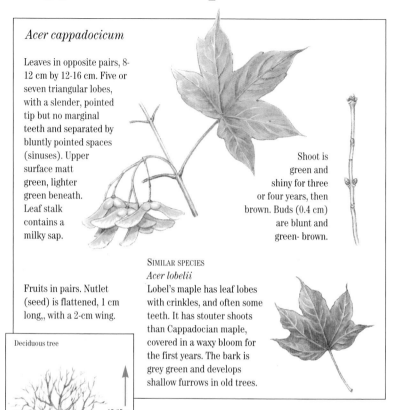

Acer cappadocicum

Leaves in opposite pairs, 8-12 cm by 12-16 cm. Five or seven triangular lobes, with a slender, pointed tip but no marginal teeth and separated by bluntly pointed spaces (sinuses). Upper surface matt green, lighter green beneath. Leaf stalk contains a milky sap.

Shoot is green and shiny for three or four years, then brown. Buds (0.4 cm) are blunt and green- brown.

Fruits in pairs. Nutlet (seed) is flattened, 1 cm long,, with a 2-cm wing.

SIMILAR SPECIES
Acer lobelii
Lobel's maple has leaf lobes with crinkles, and often some teeth. It has stouter shoots than Cappadocian maple, covered in a waxy bloom for the first years. The bark is grey green and develops shallow furrows in old trees.

Deciduous tree

15-25 m

This maple is native to eastern Turkey and the Caucasus region east to northern Iran. 'Cappadocian' comes from the province of the same name in central Turkey. Some sources also claim that the native distribution includes a region from the western Himalayas east into central China. There are similar trees here, differing in the smaller and much deeper lobes, no root suckers and much more deeply-fissured bark. These plants are often listed as sub-species *sinensis*, but they probably represent a separate species. Cappadocian maple is fairly common as an ornamental tree: the flowers are not showy, but the autumn colour of the leaves is the clearest butter yellow, perhaps matched only by ginkgo (page 14). The common form in cultivation is the cultivar 'Rubrum' which has reddish leaves when young. Less common is 'Aureum', with pale yellow to gold leaves. The tree's ability to produce suckers from the roots is unique amongst the maples.

Lobel's maple is native to southern Italy. It has a narrow, upright crown and is planted in streets and parks. The bloomed shoots add interest.

Cappadocian maple makes a small- to medium-sized tree with a rounded crown. It is surrounded by suckers from the root system. Shown here is the cultivar 'Aureum'.

BARK
Grey and somewhat roughened.

Field maple

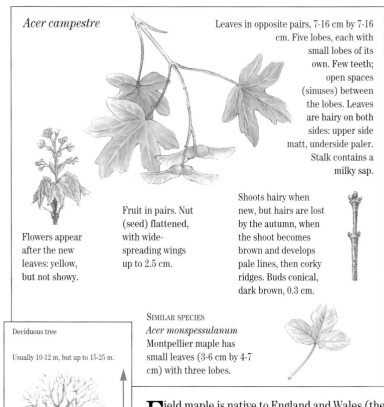

Acer campestre

Leaves in opposite pairs, 7-16 cm by 7-16 cm. Five lobes, each with small lobes of its own. Few teeth; open spaces (sinuses) between the lobes. Leaves are hairy on both sides: upper side matt, underside paler. Stalk contains a milky sap.

Flowers appear after the new leaves: yellow, but not showy.

Fruit in pairs. Nut (seed) flattened, with wide-spreading wings up to 2.5 cm.

Shoots hairy when new, but hairs are lost by the autumn, when the shoot becomes brown and develops pale lines, then corky ridges. Buds conical, dark brown, 0.3 cm.

Deciduous tree

Usually 10-12 m, but up to 15-25 m.

SIMILAR SPECIES
Acer monspessulanum
Montpellier maple has small leaves (3-6 cm by 4-7 cm) with three lobes.

Field maple is native to England and Wales (the only maple with this distinction) south into north-eastern Spain and across southern Europe to northern Turkey and the Caucasus. It is native to Denmark, but absent from the rest of Scandinavia; also to a small area in North Africa. The tree has a durable reddish wood suitable for turnery, but not available in large sizes. As with other maples, the foliage has been used for animal fodder. These days, the species is quite popular as an ornamental, because of its attractive yellow autumn colour. It grows on a wide range of sites. Field maple can be used to make hedges and withstands clipping. The new growth following clipping is often purple or pink for a few days, adding to the colour of a trimmed hedgerow.

Montpellier maple is native to Southern Europe, (except for western Spain and Portugal) east into Turkey and the Caucasus; also to North Africa. It is adapted to hot climates. Although the tree has some similarity with field maple, it is not closely related. The sap in the leaf stalk is watery, not milky. 'Monspessulanum' is the Latin name for Montpellier in southern France.

Field maple is typical of hedgerows rather than woods. It is often seen as a multi-stemmed tree, but can be drawn up to a height if sheltered by other trees.

BARK
Grey brown and pale, becoming darker on old trees and developing small scaly squares or flakes.

Japanese maple

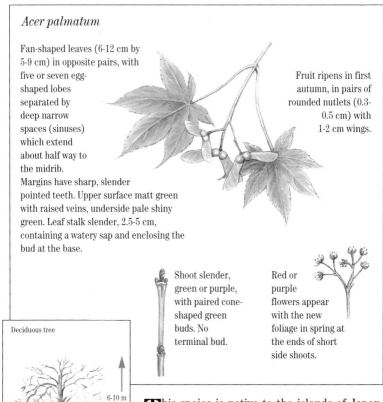

Acer palmatum

Fan-shaped leaves (6-12 cm by 5-9 cm) in opposite pairs, with five or seven egg-shaped lobes separated by deep narrow spaces (sinuses) which extend about half way to the midrib.
Margins have sharp, slender pointed teeth. Upper surface matt green with raised veins, underside pale shiny green. Leaf stalk slender, 2.5-5 cm, containing a watery sap and enclosing the bud at the base.

Fruit ripens in first autumn, in pairs of rounded nutlets (0.3-0.5 cm) with 1-2 cm wings.

Shoot slender, green or purple, with paired cone-shaped green buds. No terminal bud.

Red or purple flowers appear with the new foliage in spring at the ends of short side shoots.

Deciduous tree

6-10 m

This speies is native to the islands of Japan, where it is mainly found in the mountains. It is also native to the mainland of Asia in Korea, and north-eastern and central China. It is a popular garden ornamental, boating brilliant autumn colours: red, orange or clear yellow. The Japanese have valued it for centuries and selected many forms. These include forms with cut or dissected leaves, forms with purple leaves, normal green-leaved forms and dwarf forms with curious leaves. The cut-leaved forms make shrubs rather than trees. The purple-leaved selections with normal leaves make small trees. The purple colour is produced by an excess of the pigment xanthocyanin, which masks the normal green. Xanthocyanin is produced by most broad-leaved trees, but normally only in the new foliage; purple-leaved forms are selected to keep a higher proportion of the pigment. However, the amount of pigment retained varies, and in most purple-leaved forms the foliage becomes a dull purple-green over the summer, only reviving with the autumn colour. Some selections, such as the gorily-named (American) 'Bloodgood' stay more purple than others.

Japanese maple makes a leafy, rounded crown. Although generally small, and by nature an understorey tree (as shown here) it can grow up to 15 m in sheltered, moist sites.

BARK
Grey green, smooth with strips on young trees. On older trees it is grey or grey-brown and slightly fissured.

Silver maple

Acer saccharinum

Leaves (8-15 cm by 8-15 cm), in opposite pairs, rounded in outline. Five lobes are separated by deep narrow spaces (sinuses). Margins have coarse, often double teeth. Upper surface shiny green with raised veins; underside silvery white. Leaf stalk 5-15 cm, with a watery sap.

Fruit ripens in late spring and germinates immediately. It is set on slender, 3-5-cm stalks. Seeds have large, rounded 3-5-cm wings.

Shoot is green but with pink rings around the paired leaves in the first year, ripening to brown or purplish brown. Buds (to 1 cm) are pointed and slightly angular, red or green.

Red or greenish-red flowers hang down from lateral buds when the tree is leafless in early spring.

SIMILAR SPECIES
Acer saccharum

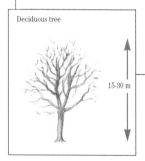

Deciduous tree

15-30 m

Sugar maple has leaves similar to Norway maple (page 228), but without the large, bristle-tipped teeth. The sap in the leaf stalk is watery, rather than milky.

Silver maple is native to eastern North America; its northern limit is Minnesota and southern Ontario, and east to New Brunswick. Its southern limit is northern Florida and eastern Oklahoma.

In Britain and Europe it makes a fast-growing ornamental tree. The branches, however, are brittle: they are especially prone to damage by wind in late summer when carrying a full crop of leaves. The fruit ripens in late spring: an adaptation to the swampy bottomland sites it occupies in the wild. These are waterlogged during autumn and winter, when most trees shed their seeds. They dry out during late spring and retain sufficient moisture to allow the seeds to get established before the autumn rains.

Sugar maple is the main tree tapped for maple syrup and is the emblem on Canada's national flag. Trees store energy reserves as sugars in the roots and trunk, which in spring are transported to the twigs as sap to make new leaves. This sap contains around 2.5 per cent sugar. Once collected, it is concentrated by boiling. Red maple (not illustrated) is very closely related to silver maple. It has a stronger, mainly red, autumn colour.

Silver maple makes a large, fast-growing tree for parks and open spaces. The crown becomes a tall, round dome.

BARK
Silver grey and smooth. On old trees, fissured and thick scaled, often with suckers at the base.

Wild service tree

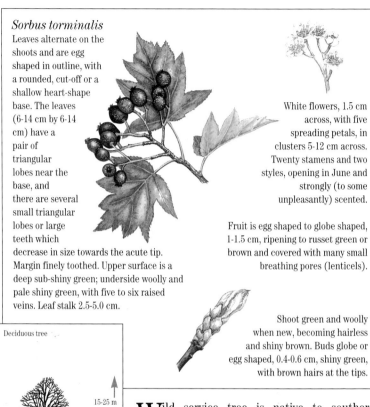

Sorbus torminalis
Leaves alternate on the shoots and are egg shaped in outline, with a rounded, cut-off or a shallow heart-shape base. The leaves (6-14 cm by 6-14 cm) have a pair of triangular lobes near the base, and there are several small triangular lobes or large teeth which decrease in size towards the acute tip. Margin finely toothed. Upper surface is a deep sub-shiny green; underside woolly and pale shiny green, with five to six raised veins. Leaf stalk 2.5-5.0 cm.

White flowers, 1.5 cm across, with five spreading petals, in clusters 5-12 cm across. Twenty stamens and two styles, opening in June and strongly (to some unpleasantly) scented.

Fruit is egg shaped to globe shaped, 1-1.5 cm, ripening to russet green or brown and covered with many small breathing pores (lenticels).

Shoot green and woolly when new, becoming hairless and shiny brown. Buds globe or egg shaped, 0.4-0.6 cm, shiny green, with brown hairs at the tips.

Deciduous tree

15-25 m

Wild service tree is native to southern England; it extends across Central and Southern Europe into Morocco and Algeria, also occurring in Turkey, although from eastern Turkey into the Caucasus and northern Iran a different form occurs, variously treated as a variety or as a separate species. Wild service tree is very different from any other species in the genus *Sorbus* and often can be treated as if in its own genus, *Torminaria*. The lobing of the leaves is more similar to some of the hawthorns (*Crataegus*) than to a *Sorbus*. The fruits are edible when fully ripe, but gritty before then. The specific name, *torminalis*, refers to the plant's role in treating colic and dysentery. The timber is useful for musical instruments, cabinets and similar items where small pieces need fitting together. It is not available in large sizes, or any quantity. Wild service tree will sucker from the roots and, in England at least, this is a major means of reproduction. (Suckers have been measured at a distance from the trunk of twice the tree's height.) The tree has hybridized with other *Sorbus* species, especially *S. aria*, to make trees such as *S. intermedia*.

Wild service tree is an occasional tree of woods and hedgerows, but rarely occurs in any great numbers. The crown becomes domed in old trees.

BARK
Smooth dark brown or grey on young trees. As the tree matures, it develops fissures and shallow, scaly plates.

Rowan

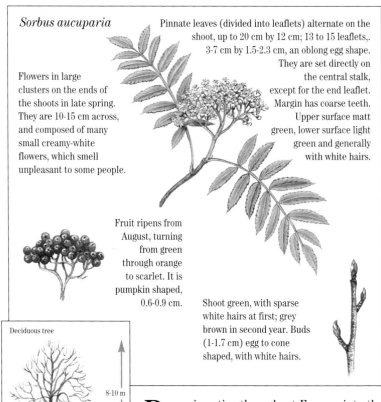

Sorbus aucuparia

Pinnate leaves (divided into leaflets) alternate on the shoot, up to 20 cm by 12 cm; 13 to 15 leaflets,. 3-7 cm by 1.5-2.3 cm, an oblong egg shape. They are set directly on the central stalk, except for the end leaflet. Margin has coarse teeth. Upper surface matt green, lower surface light green and generally with white hairs.

Flowers in large clusters on the ends of the shoots in late spring. They are 10-15 cm across, and composed of many small creamy-white flowers, which smell unpleasant to some people.

Fruit ripens from August, turning from green through orange to scarlet. It is pumpkin shaped, 0.6-0.9 cm.

Shoot green, with sparse white hairs at first; grey brown in second year. Buds (1-1.7 cm) egg to cone shaped, with white hairs.

Deciduous tree

8-10 m

Rowan is native throughout Europe, into the Caucasus and south into North Africa's Atlas Mountains. It is also native across Siberia into China, but the situation is complicated: generally, trees east of Siberia are treated as related species, but some botanists have them as subspecies. The few scattered rowans on mountain tops in Madeira are also treated as a separate species or subspecies.

The name rowan is probably derived from the Norse name for the tree. It is also called mountain ash, because the leaves are pinnate (divided into leaflets) as in ash (page 244), and because it is often the last tree, with white birch (page 114), up a hillside before the treeline. Rowan is planted as an ornamental tree in parks gardens and streets. It is used in forestry as a small broadleaved tree, especially at the margins of plantations in order to soften their regimented appearance and to attract birds and other wildlife. The fruits are attractive to birds and small mammals, and usually stripped from the trees before autumn. They can be used to make a jelly, but the seeds should be removed. As with other species in the apple family, these contain cyanide.

Rowan is characteristic of Moorland, but also occurs in lowland broadleaved and conifer forest. It has an upright, rather conical habit, but older trees are more rounded.

BARK
Smooth shiny grey or silvery grey, becoming browner on old trees and forming scaly ridges at the base.

Service tree

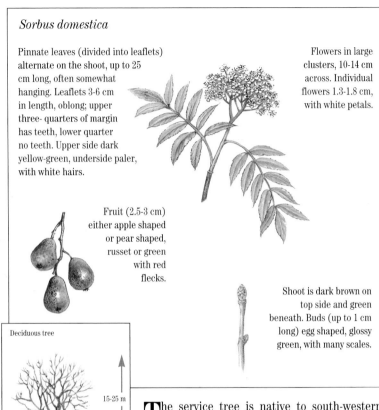

Sorbus domestica

Pinnate leaves (divided into leaflets) alternate on the shoot, up to 25 cm long, often somewhat hanging. Leaflets 3-6 cm in length, oblong; upper three- quarters of margin has teeth, lower quarter no teeth. Upper side dark yellow-green, underside paler, with white hairs.

Flowers in large clusters, 10-14 cm across. Individual flowers 1.3-1.8 cm, with white petals.

Fruit (2.5-3 cm) either apple shaped or pear shaped, russet or green with red flecks.

Shoot is dark brown on top side and green beneath. Buds (up to 1 cm long) egg shaped, glossy green, with many scales.

Deciduous tree

15-25 m

The service tree is native to south-western France east across southern Europe to the Caucasus and into Turkey; also to Morocco and Algeria in North Africa. There was a long-running debate as to whether the species was native to southern Britain. An old tree (now dead) in Wyre Forest provided the main reason for treating it as native. However, in the early 1990s, a number of shrubs on cliffs in South Wales were studied closely (as opposed to being viewed at a distance). They proved to be service trees, and not rowan as had been thought. These plants (restricted by the habitat to a small size) were natural, not plant-ed, and confirmed that the species is a native, though rare, of southern Britain.

Service tree is superficially very similar to rowan in the foliage but not relat-ed in its fruit and flower characteristics. The bark is similar to wild service tree (page 238) and the fruit contains gritty cells, as found in pears. It is some-thing of a loner in the genus *Sorbus*, and would fit better in its own genus *Cormus*. In fact, some authorities call it *Cormus domestica*. The fruit is bit-ter when first ripe; it becomes soft and sweet when over-ripe.

Service tree makes a medium to large tree with a domed crown set on spreading branches. It is usually found in broadleaved woodland.

BARK
Pale brown or brown and orange. As the tree matures, it fissures and breaks into rectangular scales.

243

Ash

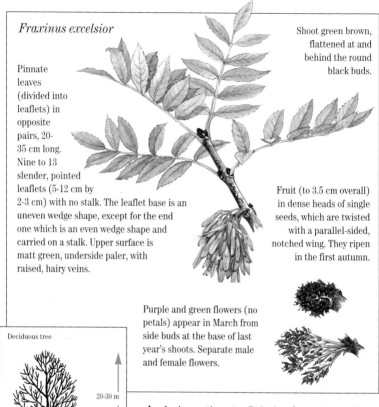

Fraxinus excelsior

Shoot green brown, flattened at and behind the round black buds.

Pinnate leaves (divided into leaflets) in opposite pairs, 20-35 cm long. Nine to 13 slender, pointed leaflets (5-12 cm by 2-3 cm) with no stalk. The leaflet base is an uneven wedge shape, except for the end one which is an even wedge shape and carried on a stalk. Upper surface is matt green, underside paler, with raised, hairy veins.

Fruit (to 3.5 cm overall) in dense heads of single seeds, which are twisted with a parallel-sided, notched wing. They ripen in the first autumn.

Purple and green flowers (no petals) appear in March from side buds at the base of last year's shoots. Separate male and female flowers.

Deciduous tree

20-30 m

Ash is native to Britain (except northern Scotland), Norway, and Sweden; also south to northern Spain and east across Central and Southern Europe to northern Turkey and the Caucasus. It grows at higher elevations than most other large broadleaved trees, and tolerates poor soils. The best examples are found in lowland forest, where on rich, clay loams over chalk they can quickly make large trees. The timber is white, valuable and resilient, used for handles of tools, flooring and panelling; it takes stain well. The wood will burn adequately when fresh and green, although it is better dried for a summer. The pinnate leaves, with many small leaflets, allow light to penetrate through the crown, so the tree only produces a light shade.

Ash has produced a number of cultivars, including several weeping forms and one ('Jaspidea') with golden twigs. The most confusing form is 'Diversifolia', which has only a single leaflet, or (rarely) three to five leaflets. The distinctive rounded black buds on shoots flattened at the nodes show this form to be an ash, and not some other species.

Ash is a common tree of hedgerows, woods and river banks. The pinnate leaves (see opposite) give a light shade, but the aggressive surface roots restrict the growth of understorey plants. The tree has a fibrous surface root system which dries out the topsoil in its vicinity, and competes hard for water and nutrients to the detriment of other plants.

BARK
Grey or grey brown, smooth on young trees, but developing interweaving fissures on old trees.

Manna ash

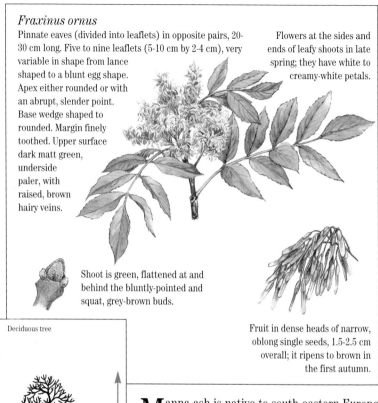

Fraxinus ornus

Pinnate eaves (divided into leaflets) in opposite pairs, 20-30 cm long. Five to nine leaflets (5-10 cm by 2-4 cm), very variable in shape from lance shaped to a blunt egg shape. Apex either rounded or with an abrupt, slender point. Base wedge shaped to rounded. Margin finely toothed. Upper surface dark matt green, underside paler, with raised, brown hairy veins.

Flowers at the sides and ends of leafy shoots in late spring; they have white to creamy-white petals.

Shoot is green, flattened at and behind the bluntly-pointed and squat, grey-brown buds.

Deciduous tree

15-25 m

Fruit in dense heads of narrow, oblong single seeds, 1.5-2.5 cm overall; it ripens to brown in the first autumn.

Manna ash is native to south-eastern Europe and around the Mediterranean and Black Sea coasts of western Turkey: an area of hot, dry summers and wet winters. It belongs to a small section of the ash genus which has petals in the flowers. By any standard, it is attractive in flower, but, compared with ash and narrow-leaved ash, it is outstanding and fully deserves its alternative common name, flowering ash. The grey-brown buds, rounded, but ending in a point, provide an easy way to separate it from ash and narrow-leaved ash all year.

Manna ash can be tapped to produce a sugar: slits are made in the bark of young trees; sap runs out and congeals on exposure to air. It is very sweet. One of the sugars it contains is mannitol, commonly used as a mild laxative. There is probably no truth in the legend that the sap was the manna which nourished the Israelites in the Sinai Desert: the tree does not grow there. The timber is similar to that of ash, and used for the same purposes. Manna ash is often grafted on to ash rootstocks, in order to produce a saleable plant quickly. However, the bark of manna ash is quite different from that of ash.

Manna ash makes a showy tree in May when laden with the creamy-white flowers. Both old and young trees have domed crowns.

BARK
Dark grey and smooth, developing weak fissures at the base.

247

Narrow-leaved ash

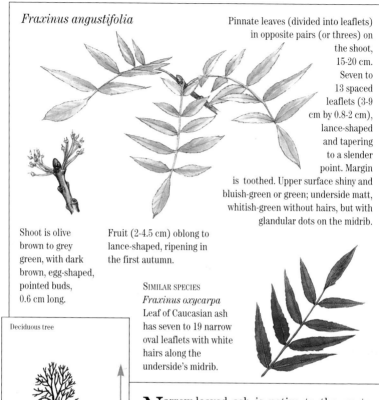

Fraxinus angustifolia

Pinnate leaves (divided into leaflets) in opposite pairs (or threes) on the shoot, 15-20 cm. Seven to 13 spaced leaflets (3-9 cm by 0.8-2 cm), lance-shaped and tapering to a slender point. Margin is toothed. Upper surface shiny and bluish-green or green; underside matt, whitish-green without hairs, but with glandular dots on the midrib.

Shoot is olive brown to grey green, with dark brown, egg-shaped, pointed buds, 0.6 cm long.

Fruit (2-4.5 cm) oblong to lance-shaped, ripening in the first autumn.

SIMILAR SPECIES
Fraxinus oxycarpa
Leaf of Caucasian ash has seven to 19 narrow oval leaflets with white hairs along the underside's midrib.

Deciduous tree

15-30 m

Narrow-leaved ash is native to the western Mediterranean region east to central Southern Europe and to Morocco and Algeria in North Africa. Small leaves or small leaflets generally give a light crown casting dappled shade; but although narrow-leaved ash's leaflets are spaced, their large number gives dense shade. The opposite leaves and buds of *Fraxinus* help to separate it from other trees with pinnate leaves, such as rowan; they are often in threes on the more vigorous shoots, and only in pairs on the weaker ones. The cultivar 'Velthamii' has leaves reduced to a single large leaflet. It is similar to the single-leaved form of ash (page 244), but can be identified by the coarse toothing, the bark, and the bud, which is dark brown to blackish grey, not black.

Caucasian ash is native to south-eastern Europe east into the Caucasus. Botanically, it is very close to narrow-leaved ash and sometimes regarded as the same. It is mainly cultivated in the 'Raywood' form which has smooth grey bark and a leafy, rounded crown. In autumn the foliage turns plum purple, whereas most ashes manage no more than a good yellow (if they turn at all).

Narrow-leaved ash has a dense, rounded crown with many small leaflets. Some trees in gardens are grafted on to ash (page 244) above ground level so that the contrast between the different barks is pronounced – as seen here in the shaded base portion of the trunk.

BARK
Dark grey to black, becoming deeply fissured into small squares. Very old trees are often knobbly.

Walnut

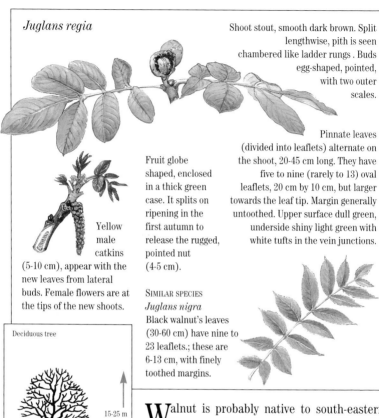

Juglans regia

Shoot stout, smooth dark brown. Split lengthwise, pith is seen chambered like ladder rungs . Buds egg-shaped, pointed, with two outer scales.

Pinnate leaves (divided into leaflets) alternate on the shoot, 20-45 cm long. They have five to nine (rarely to 13) oval leaflets, 20 cm by 10 cm, but larger towards the leaf tip. Margin generally untoothed. Upper surface dull green, underside shiny light green with white tufts in the vein junctions.

Fruit globe shaped, enclosed in a thick green case. It splits on ripening in the first autumn to release the rugged, pointed nut (4-5 cm).

Yellow male catkins (5-10 cm), appear with the new leaves from lateral buds. Female flowers are at the tips of the new shoots.

SIMILAR SPECIES
Juglans nigra
Black walnut's leaves (30-60 cm) have nine to 23 leaflets.; these are 6-13 cm, with finely toothed margins.

Deciduous tree

15-25 m

Walnut is probably native to south-eastern Europe east into Central Asia and along the Himalayas into south-western China. However, it has a long history of being cultivated for its nuts, so it may not be native throughout the entire region. Nonetheless, it forms extensive pure forests in the states of the former Soviet Union (such as Azerbaijan) in Central Asia and is almost certainly native to this region. It is very clearly an introduced tree in Britain and Western Europe, despite often being called English walnut. Apart from the nuts, it is valued for its dark-brown, richly-veined wood, long used for veneers and gun butts. In 1709, a severe winter destroyed most of the walnuts in Europe. From them on, the substitute (darker, straight-grained) black walnut was imported from North America. So genuine 'English walnut' furniture (the wood ages to a beautiful light golden colour) generally pre-dates 1709.

Black walnut is native to eastern North America from New England and South Dakota south to Florida and Texas. The leaves are larger than *Juglans regia's,* more even in size, and finely toothed.

Walnut makes a domed crown, usually with branches radiating out from a short bole or trunk. It does not tolerate shade. The tree produces chemicals which inhibit the growth of other plants.

BARK
On young trees shiny, smooth and grey, developing smooth, broad ridges separated by wide, and deep fissures.

Caucasian wingnut

Pterocarya fraxinifolia

Shoot is smooth and brown. If split lengthwise, the pith is seen chambered like the rungs of a ladder. Buds have naked, miniature leaves, but not scales.

Yellow male catkins (5-12 cm) appear with the new leaves. Fruit is a hanging (25-50-cm) catkin. Nuts (1 cm) have two rounded wings.

Pinnate leaves (divided into leaflets) alternate on the shoot, 20-50 cm, usually with 15-21 leaflets. Leaflets 5-12 cm by 4-5 cm, oblong and tapering to an acute tip, increasing in size towards it. Margin has irregular, rounded teeth; upper surface matt green, underside shiny light green, with scattered black dots.

SIMILAR SPECIES
Pterocarya stenoptera
Leaf of Chinese wingnut has finely toothed margins and the leaf stalk between the pairs of leaflets has broad wings or flanges.

Deciduous tree

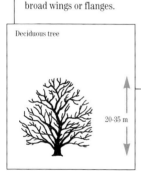

20-35 m

Carya ovata
A hickory leaf has five leaflets; the three at the end are much larger. Male catkins are in threes on a common stalk. Fruit splits along four sutures.

Caucasian wingnut is native to the Caspian forests of northern Iran and to the Caucasus. In Europe it is planted as a specimen tree and is quick-growing, with a useful timber, well adapted to moist soils. *Pterocarya* and 'wingnut' both refer to the fruit: *ptero* is from the Greek for wing and *carya* is the generic name of the related hickories. The paired wings on the nut assist in seed dispersal. *Pterocarya* has a chambered pith similar to walnut's, and is easily separated from hickory on this characteristic alone.

The three genera (illustrated above) are closely related. Chinese wingnut is native to China and extends into northern Vietnam. It is closely related to Caucasian wingnut, but differs in the longer and narrower wings on the fruit, and in not producing root suckers. The hickories, genus *Carya*, are native to North America and China. Unlike walnut and wingnut, the male catkins are set in threes on a common stalk. Their timber is very resilient to sudden shocks and widely used for tool handles. As with walnuts, but not wingnuts, the nuts are generally edible: the best is the pecan, *Carya illinoinensis*.

A single Caucasian wingnut is usually a forest – it suckers profusely from the roots. The tree is attractive for much of the summer, with its hanging fruits. The foliage turns yellow in autumn.

BARK
Dull grey, smooth on young trees, then developing criss-crossing shallow fissures and ridges.

Varnish tree

Rhus verniciflua

Large (30-60 cm) pinnate leaves (divided into leaflets) alternate on the shoot. There are seven to 19 spaced, broad egg-shaped leaflets (10-20 cm by 5-10 cm); slender pointed tips and an untoothed margin. Upper surface a lustrous fresh green, underside velvety, with short down, especially on the 16-30 pairs of veins.

Shoot is stout and pale grey, roughened by raised breathing pores. Buds (to 1 cm) egg shaped, beaked and chestnut brown.

Fruit (0.8 cm). a shiny creamy brown to yellow colour. It is flattened, with a dry, fleshy layer.

SIMILAR SPECIES
Rhus typhina
Stag's horn sumach has lance-shaped leaflets with sharply toothed margins. The flowers and fruits are carried in dense red clusters at the ends of the branches.

Deciduous tree

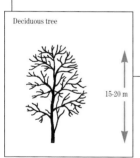

15-20 m

Varnish tree is native along the Himalayas from India east into China, occuring on dry valley bottom sites. It may also be native to other regions of south-eastern Asia and Japan, or it may be an early introduction.

The sap in the bark is harvested to make the lacquer used to varnish furniture and ornaments in Japan and the Far East. Shallow V-shaped slits are made in the bark and the sap collected in small vessels. The bark photograph opposite shows a tree in south-eastern Tibet which has been harvested for lacquer. The sap contains a number of complex chemicals, including urushiol. These are quickly absorbed by the skin and attach to body cells. After about a week, painful blistering develops – a result of the body's 'defence cells' (T-cells) attempting to eliminate contaminated matter.

Stag's horn sumach is native to eastern North America, where it forms a small tree, 5-10 metres in height and width. It suckers from the roots and, like varnish tree, has brilliant autumn colour. The shoots are stout and hairy, rather like young antlers in velvet.

Varnish tree forms an upright, domed crown when mature, but is conical and spiky when young. The glossy green foliage develops a brilliant red autumn colour.

BARK
Dark grey to buff brown, becoming fissured and somewhat scaly on old trees. The cuts seen in this photograph were made to draw out sap for varnish – see main text opposite.

Tree of Heaven

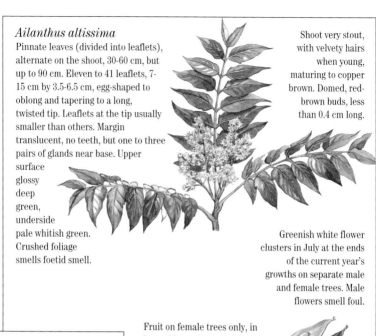

Ailanthus altissima
Pinnate leaves (divided into leaflets), alternate on the shoot, 30-60 cm, but up to 90 cm. Eleven to 41 leaflets, 7-15 cm by 3.5-6.5 cm, egg-shaped to oblong and tapering to a long, twisted tip. Leaflets at the tip usually smaller than others. Margin translucent, no teeth, but one to three pairs of glands near base. Upper surface glossy deep green, underside pale whitish green. Crushed foliage smells foetid smell.

Shoot very stout, with velvety hairs when young, maturing to copper brown. Domed, red-brown buds, less than 0.4 cm long.

Greenish white flower clusters in July at the ends of the current year's growths on separate male and female trees. Male flowers smell foul.

Fruit on female trees only, in large, 30-cm clusters with many seeds which are set in the middle of a twisted bright red or green 3.5-4.0 cm wing.

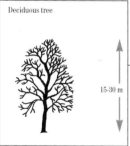

Deciduous tree

15-30 m

Tree of heaven is native to northern China, but widely cultivated in Britain and Europe for its bold foliage. It tolerates poor soils and polluted atmosphere and can be attractive when in fruit, especially if the tree has bright red wings to the seeds. It will sucker from the roots – often, suckers pop up through drain covers. The branches are somewhat brittle. The wood is soft and used for pulp.

The genus *Ailanthus*, consisting of some half dozen species, is native from India and China south through south-eastern Asia to Australia. Both tree of heaven's common and scientific names have their origin in the Moluccan name for the species, which translates either as 'very tall' or 'reaching the heavens'. The leaves have glands on the margin near the base. These are extra-floral nectaries, that is, nectaries which are not part of the flowers. Their purpose is to make sugary secretions (nectar), which are harvested by ants. In return, the ants keep caterpillars and other leaf-eating insects away from the leaves. The leaves, shoots and flowers, especially the male flowers, have an unpleasant foetid odour, although usually these are above nose level.

Tree of Heaven makes a rounded crown on a long bole, with bold foliage. It is planted as an ornamental in parks, streets and public gardens.

BARK
Smooth, grey brown to dark brown, with white streaks on young trees, developing shallow buff or grey fissures.

Box elder

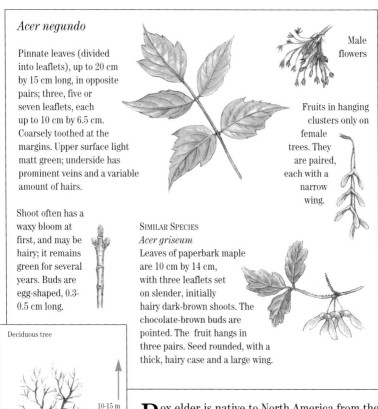

Acer negundo

Pinnate leaves (divided into leaflets), up to 20 cm by 15 cm long, in opposite pairs; three, five or seven leaflets, each up to 10 cm by 6.5 cm. Coarsely toothed at the margins. Upper surface light matt green; underside has prominent veins and a variable amount of hairs.

Male flowers

Fruits in hanging clusters only on female trees. They are paired, each with a narrow wing.

Shoot often has a waxy bloom at first, and may be hairy; it remains green for several years. Buds are egg-shaped, 0.3-0.5 cm long.

SIMILAR SPECIES
Acer griseum
Leaves of paperbark maple are 10 cm by 14 cm, with three leaflets set on slender, initially hairy dark-brown shoots. The chocolate-brown buds are pointed. The fruit hangs in three pairs. Seed rounded, with a thick, hairy case and a large wing.

Deciduous tree

10-15 m

Box elder is native to North America from the Atlantic coast to California. It is neither a box (*Buxus* species are shrubs or, rarely, small trees); or an elder (see page 281). It is, in fact, a maple and is also known as ash-leaved maple, a slightly more descriptive name. During spring it has 15 minutes of glory when the flowers, especially on male trees, hang attractively beneath the leafless boughs. Otherwise, it is rather uninspiring. There are several variegated forms, which can look attractive as shrubs.

Paperbark maple is native to central China. It makes a wonderful small tree, usually 6 to 8 m in height, but occasionally taller if located on a sheltered, fertile site. The bark is red-brown, copper or chestnut and peels in paper-thin sheets to reveal a bloomed orange colour beneath. It starts peeling on trunks and branches after they are three or four years old, at which point the colour extends up into the crown. In autumn, the leaves turn brilliant crimson, red and orange: a display equal to the best. There are inconspicuous yellow flowers. The tree thrives on a wide range of sites, but is rather slow growing.

Box elder usually makes a small, flat-topped tree with spreading branches. Illustrated here is a variegated tree.

BARK
Grey brown and smooth, becoming darker, with shallow fissures and cracks.

Carob

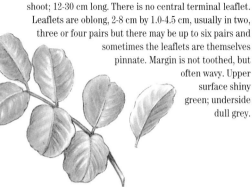

Ceratonia siliqua

Pinnate leaves (divided into leaflets) alternate on the shoot; 12-30 cm long. There is no central terminal leaflet. Leaflets are oblong, 2-8 cm by 1.0-4.5 cm, usually in two, three or four pairs but there may be up to six pairs and sometimes the leaflets are themselves pinnate. Margin is not toothed, but often wavy. Upper surface shiny green; underside dull grey.

Brown flowers in clusters of 20 to 60, carried from July to November on the older branches or on the trunk. They generally appear on separate male and female trees.

Shoot is grey, slender and hairy when young.

Fruit is an oblong pod, 10-30 cm by 1.5-3.5 cm, ripening to brown. It contains a sweet, jelly-like pulp and ten to 16 glossy brown seeds.

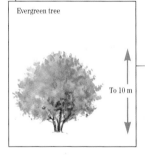

Evergreen tree

To 10 m

Carob is widely grown around, and restricted to, the shores of the Mediterranean – but it is not clear where the tree is native and where its range has been extended by cultivation. It is probably native to the eastern Mediterranean region, with Turkey or Palestine as the most likely origins. It thrives on hot, dry sites, and cannot tolerate th winter cold of Northern Europe. The tree is also known as locust. References in the Bible to John the Baptist and other prophets 'eating locusts and wild honey' refer to this tree, and not the insect – which can cause plagues. The pulp surrounding the seeds within the pods is sweet and nutritious. The pods are mainly used as cattle fodder, or to provide a gum used in paper manufacture. The seeds (used as a chocolate substitute) are of a fairly constant weight – about a fifth of a gramme, and once served as measures. The weight of diamonds and the purity of gold are still expressed in carats. The generic name is from the Greek word *keras* meaning 'horn' and probably refers to the very thick, hard coat which protects the seeds. Human fingernails are made of keratin, which has the same chemical basis.

Carob makes a small tree with a flat, spreading crown.

BARK
Brown and ridged, often with flowers or fruits growing directly from the trunk.

Robinia

Robinia pseudoacacia

Pinnate leaves (divided into leaflets) alternate on the shoot, 15-30 cm long, with nine to 19 oval leaflets 2.5-6 cm long. These have a small bristle in the notched tip, but are not toothed on the margin. Upper surface blue-green to yellow-green, underside grey-green, at first hairy on both sides. Leaf stalk base encloses the bud.

Fragrant white flowers (like pea's) appar in June. They hang in clusters 10-20 cm long at the ends of the current year's shoots.

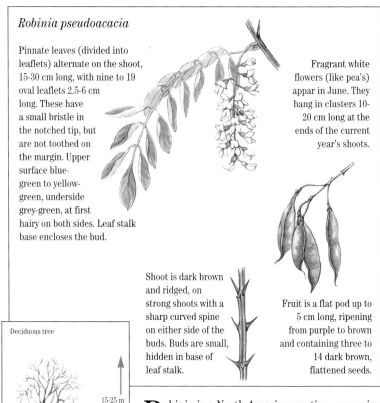

Shoot is dark brown and ridged, on strong shoots with a sharp curved spine on either side of the buds. Buds are small, hidden in base of leaf stalk.

Fruit is a flat pod up to 5 cm long, ripening from purple to brown and containing three to 14 dark brown, flattened seeds.

Deciduous tree

15-25 m

Robinia is a North American native, occurring naturally in a triangle from Pennsylvania to Ohio and Alabama; also in a separate band from southern Missouri to eastern Oklahoma. It thrives on light sandy soils, but also grows on heavier soils, provided the site is well drained. It has become naturalized in regions with a warm summer climate. The tree produces root suckers which are usually armed with pairs of sharp spines at each bud or leaf. They are a striking feature, produced only on the vigorous growths and derived from the pair of small primitive leaves or stipules which are found beside the leaves in many broadleaved trees. Stipules tend to be found on the young shoots of species such as *Betula, Carpinus* and *Tilia*, and are quickly lost. However, they may be persistent and leafy in some trees, for example, goat willow (page 136).

Robinia is also known as false acacia, from the scientific name, while the American common name is black locust. Robinia is a member of the legume family, whose roots harbour bacteria which can make nitrogen fertilizer for the tree from air in the soil. The timber is of reasonable quality.

Robinia quickly makes a large, rugged tree with na tall, domed crown, but is rarely as old as its appearance suggests.

BARK
Smooth and brown on young trees, but quickly becoming rough and dark grey, with coarse ridges and furrows.

Pagoda tree

Sophora japonica

Pinnate leaves (divided into leaflets) alternate on the shoot. They are 15-25 cm long, with nine to 15 egg-shaped leaflets, 3-6 cm by 2-3.5 cm. Untoothed margins. Upper surface matt green, without hairs; underside bluish or whitish green, with white silky hairs.

Shoot is green for several years. Buds are small, hidden in enlarged base of the leaf stalk.

Fruit is a hairy pod, 5-8 cm long constricted between the one to six seeds.

Flowers in broad clusters at the end of the current season's growth in August-September. They are pea-shaped and creamy white, around 1.5 cm long.

Deciduous tree

15-25 m

Pagoda tree is native to northern China, where it is one of the few large broadleaved trees that can cope with the local dry winters and springs. It is possibly also a native of Japan, but the evidence suggests that it was probably introduced there when Japan embraced Buddhism. It was introduced to Britain and Europe from Japan in the 18th century. The common name refers to its planting as a shade tree in the grounds of pagodas and temples. It is usually placed in the genus *Sophora,* but modern research suggests that it should be moved to a new genus, *Styphnolobium*. It is one of the many members of the legume family which have flowers like a pea's. They comprise five petals arranged with two 'keels' at the base, a 'wing' on each side and a 'standard' which acts like an umbrella over the top. *Cercis* (page 202), robinia (page 262) and laburnum (page 281) also have this type of flower. Pagoda tree needs a hot sunny summer to set the flower buds. In dull or wet summers the floral display is much poorer, while young trees generally do not flower. It is useful as a specimen tree for flowering late in the summer, but has no autumn colour.

Pagoda tree makes a domed crown. The green leaves act as a foil for the creamy-white flowers in late summer.

BARK
Dark brown or grey, folded or broadly ridged.

Honey locust

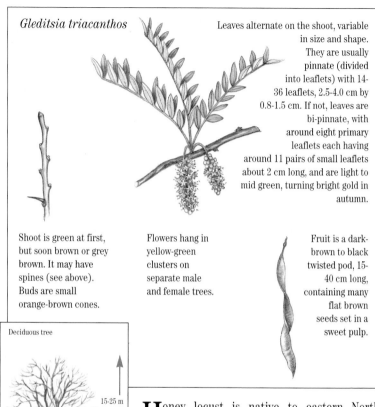

Gleditsia triacanthos

Leaves alternate on the shoot, variable in size and shape. They are usually pinnate (divided into leaflets) with 14-36 leaflets, 2.5-4.0 cm by 0.8-1.5 cm. If not, leaves are bi-pinnate, with around eight primary leaflets each having around 11 pairs of small leaflets about 2 cm long, and are light to mid green, turning bright gold in autumn.

Shoot is green at first, but soon brown or grey brown. It may have spines (see above). Buds are small orange-brown cones.

Flowers hang in yellow-green clusters on separate male and female trees.

Fruit is a dark-brown to black twisted pod, 15-40 cm long, containing many flat brown seeds set in a sweet pulp.

Deciduous tree

15-25 m

Honey locust is native to eastern North America in an area bounded by South Dakota, southern Oregon to Pennsylvania in the north and northern Florida to south-eastern Texas in the south. It is appreciated for the pleasant, light, dappled shade provided by the deeply divided leaves. The tree's wild form is armed with large three-pronged spines, up to 20 cm in length. These can be on the shoots, but are also produced directly from the trunk, where they can form large clusters. They are an attractive feature, but very sharp, and can be a safety hazard if honey locusts are planted beside roads. Selective breeding has produced forms without spines, such as var. *inermis* and these are preferred for ornamental planting. The clone 'Sunburst' is part of var. *inermis*: its new foliage in the spring is golden yellow, maturing to yellow green. The sweet fleshy pulp surrounding the seeds has a purpose. The pod does not open to release the seeds: but is intended to be eaten by a large mammal. The seed's thick coat is broken down by the animal's stomach acids, and in due course the seed is planted away from the parent tree in the animal's manure.

Honey locust makes a tall tree which usually loses its lower foliage to display the trunk. The leaves turn a fine gold colour in autumn.

BARK
Blackish grey or purplish grey and rough, becoming scaly with long narrow ridges on old trees. The bark may have three pronged spines.

Silver wattle or 'mimosa'

Acacia dealbata

Bi-pinnate leaves (see honey locust, page 266), 10-15 cm by 4-6 cm, with even numbers of leaflets. The smallest divisions – 'pinnules' (0.3-04 cm) are in about 50 pairs on each of the two dozen or so pairs of larger (3-4 cm) leaflets. Leaves are grey--green, with some silky hairs, but new ones are golden brown.

In late winter, flowers open into 7-15 cm long heads from buds set the previous year. Fragrant, globe-shaped bright yellow flowers are 0.5-0.6 cm in diameter.

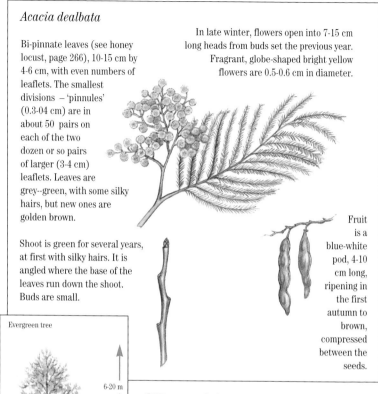

Shoot is green for several years, at first with silky hairs. It is angled where the base of the leaves run down the shoot. Buds are small.

Fruit is a blue-white pod, 4-10 cm long, ripening in the first autumn to brown, compressed between the seeds.

Evergreen tree

6-20 m

Silver wattle is native to New South Wales and Victoria in south-eastern mainland Australia; also to Tasmania. It is widely cultivated in mild areas of Europe as a winter-flowering tree; likely to be cut back by hard winters, unless killed out-right, it usually regrows either from the stump or from root suckers. The flowers are sold by florists who know it, like many people, as 'mimosa'. However, the true mimosa is a different genus and not hardy in Europe. *Acacia dealbata* belongs to the legume family, and has a typical legume fruit, but in common with *Gleditsia* and *Ceratonia,* it does not have pea-shaped flowers. The attraction of silver wattle flowers are not the petals, but the massed, showy stamens.

Acacia is a large genus, with around 1,200 different species, especially common in Australia and Africa. In Africa, they are typical trees of the savannah. Most *Acacia* species have large spines (fortunately absent in silver wattle) derived from the stipules (see robinia, page 262). Acacias are adapted to regions that have long, dry periods. Many of them cope with lack of water by not having leaves but tough, modified green shoots called phyllodes.

Silver wattle is flamboyant in late winter when the bright yellow flowers dominate the leaves. It makes a cone- or column-shaped tree and has attractive foliage.

BARK
Blue green and smooth on young trees, but becoming corrugated and chocolate brown, then grey or black on old trees.

Pride of India

Koelreuteria paniculata

Pinnate leaves (divided into leaflets) up to 45cm. Pink, reddish or yellowish when young. They have five to six pairs of leaflets which are often partially pinnate (in other words, partly bi-pinnate See honey locust, page 266.

Flowers in August form in large terminal clusters (20-40 cm) containing many rich yellow blooms with strap-like petals.

Leaflets are egg shaped, up to 8 cm by 5 cm. Margin has large rounded teeth. Upper surface is dark green, underside light green.

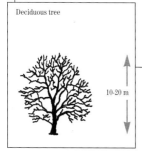

Shoot is coppery brown when young, later light brown. Buds (0.6 cm) are conical, green and brown.

Fruit is an inflated papery bladder (4-5 cm) with three sections, each with a single black or dark-brown, pea-sized seed.

Deciduous tree

10-20 m

Pride of India is native to China, Japan and Korea, but not to India. It acquired its name at a time when the terms 'India' or 'Indian' were applied to almost anything from the Orient, and many things from the west (such as the West Indies and Red Indians). Another name for the species is golden rain tree, and while the flowers can fairly be described as golden, they do not 'rain' but are carried erect above the foliage or spreading out from the ends of the shoots. The scientific name commemorates J. Koelreute, an 18th-century naturalist from Karlsbad; and the technical shape of the flower clusters, which are in a panicle (a branched or compound raceme).

Pride of India makes a welcome ornamental tree because it flowers in August, when there are few other trees in bloom. It needs a long, hot summer in order to produce the best floral display and should be sited where it can get the most light. The large leaves turn yellow in autumn, changing from purple-green to brown. The seeds rattle around in the dry papery capsules and are dispersed by the wind.

Pride of India has a rounded
crown formed from radiating
branches on a short trunk. The
large compound leaves cast
only a light shade.

BARK
Brown or purple-brown;
rough, with narrow orange
fissures.

Horse chestnut

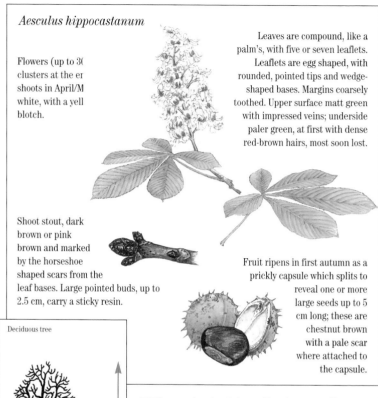

Aesculus hippocastanum

Leaves are compound, like a palm's, with five or seven leaflets. Leaflets are egg shaped, with rounded, pointed tips and wedge-shaped bases. Margins coarsely toothed. Upper surface matt green with impressed veins; underside paler green, at first with dense red-brown hairs, most soon lost.

Flowers (up to 3(clusters at the er shoots in April/M white, with a yell blotch.

Shoot stout, dark brown or pink brown and marked by the horseshoe shaped scars from the leaf bases. Large pointed buds, up to 2.5 cm, carry a sticky resin.

Fruit ripens in first autumn as a prickly capsule which splits to reveal one or more large seeds up to 5 cm long; these are chestnut brown with a pale scar where attached to the capsule.

Deciduous tree

20-35 m

Horse chestnut is native to a small area of northern Greece and southern Albania where it has survived since the most recent ice age. (When it was first introduced to Europe in the 1500s it was believed to come from Turkey.) It quickly established itself as part of Europe's tree heritage and is naturalized in Britain and other parts of Europe. The name refers to the fruits or nuts, which can be fed in small quantities to animals. To humans they are bitter and inedible – but have had a limited use in perfume manufacture. Much better known, of course, is their role in the game of conkers, which probably derives, in turn, from an earlier one using snail shells (*conches* in French).

Horse chestnut does everything in a rush in the spring – like daffodils. Adult trees rarely produce a second flush of foliage: if the first set is lost, the tree normally waits until the next spring before making any new ones. Branches with the large sticky buds make a pleasant winter decoration if stood in a vase. The wood is soft, easily split and of no real quality. Pink horse chestnut (*Aesculus carnea*) is a separate species, with darker leaves and pink flowers.

Horse chestnut has a tall, domed crown. In spring it is clothed by the large erect candles of flowers. The foliage may turn scarlet, gold, orange or a pale, dull brown in autumn.

BARK
Red-brown or grey-brown, smooth on young trees but developing thick scale; on old trees it is fissured at the base.

273

Chusan or windmill palm

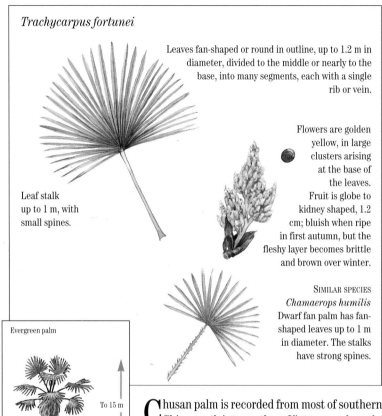

Trachycarpus fortunei

Leaves fan-shaped or round in outline, up to 1.2 m in diameter, divided to the middle or nearly to the base, into many segments, each with a single rib or vein.

Flowers are golden yellow, in large clusters arising at the base of the leaves. Fruit is globe to kidney shaped, 1.2 cm; bluish when ripe in first autumn, but the fleshy layer becomes brittle and brown over winter.

Leaf stalk up to 1 m, with small spines.

SIMILAR SPECIES
Chamaerops humilis
Dwarf fan palm has fan-shaped leaves up to 1 m in diameter. The stalks have strong spines.

Evergreen palm

To 15 m

Chusan palm is recorded from most of southern China south into northern Vietnam and northern Burma, but is unlikely to be native throughout this area. Man has been planting it for many centuries for its fibre, which is produced at the base of the leaves, wraps the trunk in a protective layer, and can be removed in small sheets – a natural unwoven cloth. The Yi minority peoples in Yunnan use it to make rainwear, wearing the sheets over the back so that they shed rain much like a thatched roof. The leaf fibres are also used for weaving. Though the hardiest of the palms, it is tender as a young plant.

Dwarf fan palm or European fan palm is native to the western Mediterranean region, where it is common in dry evergreen scrub along the western coast of Italy, southern Spain and North Africa. This is the only palm native to the mainland of Europe, but only rarely makes a tree in the wild; it can grow to 8 or 9 m in cultivation. The species is very similar to *Trachycarpus fortunei,* but easily separated by its shrub-like shape, with its several unbranched stems, and the prominent spines on the leaf stalk.

Chusan palm has only a single stem, with the leaves restricted to a tuft at the top, where live leaves spread upwards and outwards and the older dead leaves hang down.

BARK
Covered by the fibrous red-brown to dull brown bases of the leaves (see photograph), but where removed it is grey, with ridges made by the fallen leaves.

Canary palm

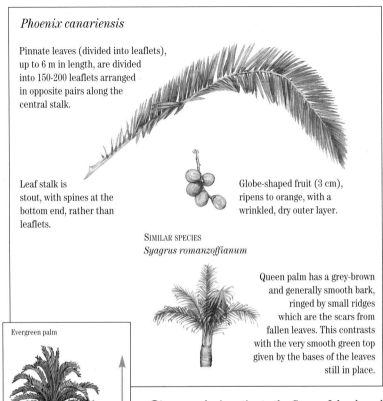

Phoenix canariensis

Pinnate leaves (divided into leaflets), up to 6 m in length, are divided into 150-200 leaflets arranged in opposite pairs along the central stalk.

Leaf stalk is stout, with spines at the bottom end, rather than leaflets.

Globe-shaped fruit (3 cm), ripens to orange, with a wrinkled, dry outer layer.

SIMILAR SPECIES
Syagrus romanzoffianum

Queen palm has a grey-brown and generally smooth bark, ringed by small ridges which are the scars from fallen leaves. This contrasts with the very smooth green top given by the bases of the leaves still in place.

Evergreen palm

15-20 m

Canary palm is native to the Canary Islands and widely planted as an ornamental tree. It can make majestic specimens, with trunks up to 0.9 m in diameter. It is closely allied to the date palm (page 278), but does not sucker: so it is a neater tree for ornamental use. However, the fruit is not edible.

Palms belong to the large group of plants known as monocots, a name derived from the term monocotyledon, which describes the single cotyledon or seed leaf produced by the germinating seed. Grasses, bamboos, orchids and bulbs such as daffodils are all monocots. A characteristic of monocots is their inability to make secondary thickening of the trunk. The full diameter has to be made as it grows: it cannot be increased, as in other trees, by later laying down new wood and bark. If a palm tree goes through a lean period, the trunk formed at this time may be thinner than the trunk above.

Queen palm is native to Brazil and Argentina and planted in mild areas as a shapely ornamental. It is sometimes put in a genus of its own as *Arecastrum romanzoffianum.*

276

Canary palm makes a striking ornamental tree with its long, finely divided leaves and stout bole.

BARK
Initially hidden by the fibrous leaf bases, but when these fall it looks grey and rough because of the leaf-base scars.

Date palm

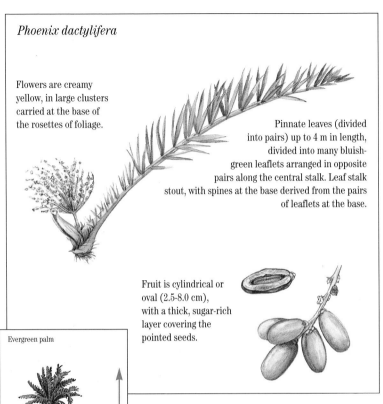

Phoenix dactylifera

Flowers are creamy yellow, in large clusters carried at the base of the rosettes of foliage.

Pinnate leaves (divided into pairs) up to 4 m in length, divided into many bluish-green leaflets arranged in opposite pairs along the central stalk. Leaf stalk stout, with spines at the base derived from the pairs of leaflets at the base.

Fruit is cylindrical or oval (2.5-8.0 cm), with a thick, sugar-rich layer covering the pointed seeds.

Evergreen palm

15-30 m

Date palm is a native of the Middle East, but has been cultivated for so many centuries that it is impossible to work out its natural distribution. It thrives in hot, dry regions provided it has access to moisture at the roots. Its fruitd -- the dates – are delicious when raw and are a staple food for many millions of people. They are easily dried when the sugar content rises to 50 per cent, allowing them to be kept for long periods. Date palm leaves are used for thatching and weaving; the trunk provides timber; and freshly-felled trees ooze a sweet sap which can be fermented to make an alcoholic drink.

In Europe the date palm is mainly grown as an ornamental in the mildest areas along the Mediterranean coast, but there are commercial plantations in a small area of south-eastern Spain. As an ornamental tree it lacks the grace and poise of the related Canary palm (page 276), having a much more slender trunk, rarely more than 0.3 m in diameter. It also produces suckers around the base of the trunk. These provide an alternate means of propagation, but are inconvenient in specimen trees planted beside boulevards.

Date palm makes a slender-trunked tree surrounded by suckers at the base.

BARK
Initially the fibrous leaf bases cover the trunk, but these fall to reveal the true bark as grey and rough – a result of scars left by fallen leaves.

Shrubs and shrub-like trees

Hoary willow
Salix elaeagnos
Deciduous; rarely to 16 m.
Shrubby, small tree

Identification The shoots have a dense grey or white covering of hairs when young, but mature to yellow- or red-brown. The leaves are 5-13 cm by 0.3-2.2cm, with fine teeth. Covered in dense hairs when new and remaining so beneath. Catkins appear with the leaves. **Distribution** Native to wet places across Central Europe from France and Spain east into the Ukraine and Turkey.

Purple osier
Salix purpurea
Deciduous; to 5 m.
Shrub or small tree

Identification Usually coppiced (cut down to ground level), in order to produce abundant flexible purple stems used in basket-making. The leaves are very slender, 3-12 cm by 0.3-0.8 cm. The flowers are catkins, produced before the leaves in spring. **Distribution** The species is widespread on wet sites throughout Europe and North Africa and extending east through Asia to China.

Almond-leaved willow
Salix triandra
Deciduous; to 10 m.
Shrubby tree

Identification The shoots are hairless, a shiny green-brown or red-brown. Leaves are 4-11 cm by 1.5-2.5 cm with coarse teeth, dark shiny green above, bluish green beneath. The male catkins appear with the leaves and have three (tri) stamens (andra). **Distribution** Almond-leaved willow is native to riverbanks across Europe and Asia, but not in the far north or far south of either continent.

Osier
Salix viminalis
Deciduous; to 10 m.
Shrubby tree.

Identification The new shoots are downy grey, but mature to yellow-green or olive-green. Leaves are densely set, 10-25 cm by 0.5-2.5 cm, with many (20-35) pairs of veins. The leaf margin is not toothed, but rolled down. Catkins appear before the leaves in spring. **Distribution** Widely planted in wet places for basketry, but only native to Central Europe; naturalized in Western Europe.

Sea buckthorn
Hippophae rhamnoides
Deciduous; to 13 m.
Suckering shrub or small tree

Elder
Sambucus nigra
Deciduous; to 10 m.
Shrub, very occasionally a small tree

Identification The stiff shoots are silvery grey and end in a sharp spine. The leaves are 2.5-7.5 cm by 0.3-0.7 cm, with untoothed margins, and covered in dense, silvery-grey scales. The fruits, only on female trees, are orange to amber, 0.6-0.9 cm and very juicy. **Distribution** Native to specific habitats, such as coastal dunes or river gravels, from Britain east to western China.

Identification Shoots are stout, with a thick pith and carry opposite pairs of pinnate leaves divided usually into five or seven 4.5-7.0 cm by 3-5 cm leaflets. Flowers are white, in large clusters at the end of shoots in mid summer, followed by purplish-black berries in autumn. Flowers and fruits can be used to flavour wines and cordials. **Distribution** Throughout Europe, North Africa and western Asia.

Cornelian cherry
Cornus mas
Deciduous; to 15 m.
Shrub or small tree

Laburnum
Laburnum anagryoides
Deciduous; 10 m.
Small tree

Identification The slender hairy shoots are green or purplish pink. Leaves are in opposite pairs, 4-10 cm by 2-4 cm, not toothed. Flowers are yellow, appearing in late winter. The fruit (1.5-2.4 cm) ripens in late summer, when it is oblong and covered by a sweet fleshy layer which can be used to make jam. **Distribution** The species is native to Southern Europe and eastern Asia.

Identification The shoots are grey-green with silky grey hairs and alternate leaves. Leaflets (3-8 cm), untoothed, with silky hairs when young. The flowers (like a pea's) are in loose, hanging clusters, 10-30 cm long. The fruit, a legume, contains black seeds which are poisonous. The timber has a black heartwood. **Distribution** The species is native to Central and Southern Europe.

Snowy mespilus
Amelanchier laevis
Deciduous; to 8 m.
Shrub or small tree

Identification The shoots are slender and olive-brown, darkening in the second year. Leaves are 2.5-5.5 cm by 1.5-3.5 cm, with sharp, triangular teeth. The white flowers are in small clusters with the new leaves in spring, followed by small, blackish-purple fruits (0.6-0.8 cm) which ripen in June or July.
Distribution Native to eastern North America, but widely naturalised in Britain and Europe.

May or hawthorn
Crataegus monogyna
Deciduous; 8-15 m.
Small tree

Identification The shoot is slender and often has sharp straight spines. The leaves (1.5-5.0 cm by 2-5 cm) have deep lobes. The white flowers, in clusters of nine to 18, appear at the ends of leafy shoots in May (hence the common name). The fruits or haws ripen to maroon in the autumn with a mealy flesh and a single seed. **Distribution** Native throughout Europe (except Iceland) east into western Asia.

Medlar
Mespilus germanica
Deciduous; 5-8 m.
Shrub or small tree

Identification The shoots have dense white hairs when young, maturing to brown; often spiny. Leaves are 5-15 cm. Flowers are single on leafy shoots in May or June and followed by the pear-shaped fruits (2-3 cm) with prominent sepals. These are sweet when fully ripe. **Distribution** Native from south-eastern Europe east into Asia as far as Iran; widely naturalized in Central Europe.

Quince
Cydonia oblonga
Deciduous; 5-8 m.
Small tree

Identification Shoots are covered in loose woolly hairs at first, but ripen to chocolate-brown. Leaves are 5-10 cm by 4-9 cm, with untoothed margins. The flowers are pink or white, at the ends of short, leafy shoots. They are followed by the golden-yellow, pear-shaped fruits (2.5-12 cm by 2-8 cm) with a delightful fragrance. **Distribution** Native through Southern Europe and east into western Asia.

282

Cherry laurel
Prunus laurocerasus
Evergreen; to 15 m.
Shrub or small tree

Plum
Prunus domestica
Deciduous; 6-10 m.
Small tree

Identification The shoot is green for the first winter, then grey-brown. The leaves are large, 8-20 cm by 3-8 cm, and arranged rather flat on the shoots, glossy green above and paler beneath. White flowers open in late winter from last year's shoots. The fruits ripen in autumn to blackish purple and have a very bitter taste. **Distribution** Native to south-eastern Europe, Turkey and Georgia.

Identification The shoots are hairy – ie they do not have spines – and lack a terminal bud. The leaves are 3-8 cm by 1.5-5 cm, with toothed margins. Flowers are white, single or in twos or threes, appearing before the leaves and followed by the juicy fruits, which may be up to 8 cm long. **Distribution** Plum is probably native only to the Caucasus region, but widely cultivated throughout the world for its fruit.

Cherry plum or Myrobalan plum
Prunus cerasifera
Deciduous; 8-12 m.
Small tree

Laurel or bay laurel
Laurus nobilis
Evergreen; to 20 m.
Shrub or tree

Identification The shoot is green for the first winter, then brown. The leaves are 4-6 cm by 2.5-3.0 cm and toothed. The flowers open white (but pink in the purple-foliaged forms) before the leaves expand. The fruit (2.5-3.0 cm) ripens in late summer. **Distribution** Uncertain origin, but probably derived as a fruit tree from a species found in the Balkans east into central Asia.

Identification Green or purplish shoots. Leaves are 5-13 cm by 2-5 cm, with a crinkled margin, strongly aromatic and used as a culinary herb. The leaves and black berries were woven into wreaths by the ancient Greeks and Romans to honour generals and poets: hence *baccalaureate*, bachelor degrees, and poet laureate. **Distribution** Native to the Mediterranean region.

Index of common and Latin names

Some of the scientific names in this index have synonyms. This is shown by 'see' and then the official scientific name. Eg *Cerasus avium* see *Prunus avium* 180

Index of common and Latin names

Index of common and Latin names

Specialist guides covering the full range of European trees

Trees of Britain & Europe Keith Rushforth, in the Collins Wildlife Trust
Series, publsihed by HarperCollins.

Trees and Shrubs Hardy in the British Isles, W. J. Bean, published by John Murray

Manual of Broadleaved Trees and Shrubs and Manual of Cultivated Conifers and, Gert
Krussman, Batsford.